World University Library

The World University Library is an international
series of books, each of which has been specially
commissioned. The authors are leading scientists and
scholars from all over the world who, in an age of
increasing specialisation, see the need for a
broad, up-to-date presentation of their subject.
The aim is to provide authoritative introductory
books for university students which will be of interest
also to the general reader.
The series is published in Britain, France, Germany,
Holland, Italy, Spain, Sweden and the United States.

Frontispiece. The coast of sw Attika seen from the Temple of
Poseidon at Sounion (*c.* 440 BC).

W.G.Forrest

The Emergence of
Greek Democracy
800–400 BC

World University Library

McGraw-Hill Book Company
New York   Toronto

Library of Congress Catalog Card Number 65-23825
Filmset by BAS Printers Limited, Wallop, Hampshire, England
Printed by Officine Grafiche Arnoldo Mondadori, Verona, Italy

Contents

Maps

The Parthenon or temple of Athena Parthenos from the NW. This, the finest of the Periklean temples, was designed by Iktinos and Kallikrates and built between 447 and 438 BC. Its decorative sculpture was supervised and partly executed by Pheidias (see figures on pages 24 and 40). In antiquity the foreground was terraced and the view would have been obscured by statues and other small shrines.

1 Failure and achievement

The failure of Athens

At the festival of Dionysos in spring, 415 BC, in the seventeenth year of the Peloponnesian War, four months after Athens had attacked and destroyed the small and comparatively innocent island of Melos, three months before a vast expedition was sent out to add Sicily to her empire, Euripides produced one of his starkest tragedies, the *Trojan Women*, a bitter study of the useless cruelty of war, destructive for the conquered and no less demoralising for the victor. Troy has fallen and its women, led by the aged queen Hekabe, wait for the Greeks' decisions on their fate: bit by bit the news is brought, Andromache, the wife of Hektor, falls to Pyrrhos, Kassandra, the virgin prophetess, has been chosen by the Commander-in-Chief, Agamemnon ('What luck to find oneself in a royal bed', says the simple-minded messenger), Andromache's infant son is to be thrown from the walls of Troy; and Hekabe herself, after sharing the agony of daughter-in-law, daughter and grandson, is led off to slavery while what is left of her city goes up in flames. The disaster is complete but the misery of it is not Euripides' only concern – in a prologue, the gods Athena and Poseidon have set it in a wider context:

Mad is the man who sacks a city; whoever makes a desert of temples and tombs, the sanctuaries of the dead, has laid up destruction for himself in time to come. (*Trojan Women*, 95–7).

The sack of Troy and the sufferings of the returning Greeks lay eight centuries in the past in 415 but no one could miss the parallel; by implication this was a condemnation alike of Athens' policy in the past and of her ambitions for the future. Only a very confident audience can stomach meat as strong as this.

Three years later, at the same tragic festival, the same author presented his *Helena*, a melodramatic fantasy of great charm and beauty but of little merit as, indeed with no pretensions as a serious dramatic work and of no immediate relevance: Helen had not eloped with Paris, she had waited innocently in Egypt

9

while her husband Menelaos fought for ten years before the walls of Troy to recover not her but a phantom, created by the gods in her image to help reduce the world's surplus population; and to Egypt Menelaos comes at last, dragging the phantom with him, just in time to save his real wife's virtue from the designs of a wicked Egyptian king. There is not much tragedy here; rather, a romantic fairy-tale, dreamed up out of hare-brained mythology and clever-clever contemporary philosophy. But the explanation of the change of tone is obvious enough.

The first expedition to Sicily had largely wasted the campaigning season of 415 but settled down at last to besiege the richest prize of all, the city of Syrakuse. There, however, a combination of ill-luck and incompetent generalship gradually lost the Athenians the initiative; the fleet found itself bottled up in the Syrakusan harbour, the army was virtually besieged on land and a huge reinforcing fleet which arrived early in the summer of 413 was only in time to share the destruction of those already there. Incredibly Athens had lost the better part of her navy and something like a third of her total military forces – in 412 Euripides' audience had no confidence left, they wanted to forget reality.

In politics as in the theatre the Athenian could not face responsibility; for the first time in over fifty years he was prepared, even anxious, to let others take decisions for him, prepared to abandon his democratic constitution and hand over power to an oligarchy. Not for long, it is true – within a year of March 412 Athenians were laughing at an Aristophanic parody of the *Helena* in his *Thesmophoriazusae*, and, within three months of the oligarchic *coup* in May 411 which put all authority in the hands of 400 men, the 400 were overthrown and the administration was made over to 'those best able to serve the state with their bodies and their resources', in fact to a body of 9,000. Even this more liberal régime had lasted only nine months or so when full democracy was restored. Yet for all this resilience, a resilience which prolonged the war for six years more, the Athens of 415 was gone, and when, in 404, a Spartan fleet sailed into the Peiraieus, it did no more than confirm what

BLACK
SEA

Epidamnos

Apollonia

Byzantion

PROPONTIS

THASOS

Potidaia

LEMNOS

Sigeion

KERKYRA

Pharai

Pagasai

AEGEAN SEA

LESBOS

Mytilene

Ambrakia

Anaktorion

LEUKAS

EUBOIA

Phokaia

KEPHALLENIA

Kalydon

Delphi

Chalkis

Eretria

CHIOS

Kolophon

Thebes

Sikyon

Megara

ATHENS

Ephesos

Elis

Korinth

ANDROS

SAMOS

Magnesia

ZAKYNTHOS

Argos

Epidauros

IKARIA

Miletos

Olympia

Sparta

NAXOS

Ialysos

RHODES

KARPATHOS

KRETE

Kydonia

Knossos

GREECE

0   100   200
                          Miles

0   100   200   300
                          Kilometres

A Trojan scene from a Korinthian mixing-bowl (*krater*; cf. figure on page 95) of the early sixth century. On the left are King Priam and Queen Hekabe; the other figures are Trojan warriors and women and, in the centre, perhaps, prisoners-of-war.

most Greeks, even most Athenians, already knew, that an extraordinary experiment in imperialism had failed.

It was impossible to separate this imperialism from the democracy which had fostered it and political morals were soon drawn. Sparta boasted that her oligarchic constitution had remained unchanged through ten generations; a stable oligarchy, then, was better than a fickle, reckless democracy. Athens' greatness had been built up in early democratic days, before the lowest class of citizen, the men who rowed her ships, had begun to make themselves felt in politics; democracy, then, was admirable so long as half the *demos*, the lower half, showed no interest in working it. Athens had still been successful even under full democracy so long as one man, the aristocrat Perikles, was there to control it; radical democracy, then, was tolerable if radical democracy meant no more than dictatorship by consent. These morals all had in common that they laid the blame for disaster firmly on the ordinary Athenian. They also had in common that they were drawn by men who were not themselves ordinary Athenians. They were partisan views, yet they have inspired most judgments passed on Athens since – and they are more or less totally false.

To the modern historian Athens between about 460 and 400 BC presents many puzzling contrasts and inconsistencies. For a considerable part of the period, 443 to 429, she was led by Perikles (born about 490, died 429), the man who for all his noble birth had helped in his early years (between 462 and 451) to complete the democratisation of the constitution; who had gone on to redefine the basis of the great alliance that Athens had formed and led against the Persians (between 478 and 449) in such a way that it became virtually an Athenian Empire; who had so prepared Athens' resources, economic and military, that by 431 no other power or collection of powers in Greece could think of challenging her at sea or force her to fight on land; who, finally, had a vision of Athens and her role in the Greek world which, as presented by Thucydides in the Funeral Speech (ii, 35–46), has worried schoolboys, excited their masters and enthralled idealistic historians ever since.

Perikles apart, these were also the years which saw the production of the last and greatest tragedies of Aeschylos, which covered most of the working life of the other great dramatists, Sophokles and Euripides, and of the comedian Aristophanes. Peace with Persia in 449 opened the way for the construction of a vast range of public buildings, sacred and profane, which included the Parthenon, the Hephaistion, the Odeion, stoas in the Agora, temples at Sounion and Rhamnous, and, a little later, the Erechtheion; some of the finest achievements of Greek architecture; alongside the architects,

This plan is compiled from various excellent drawings for different dates made by J. Travlos for the American School at Athens. Uncertainty has led to the omission of many details (statue bases, altars and the like) and the evidence of archaeology is itself too imprecise to guarantee all the detail that is given. But this is a fairly accurate picture of the main features of the commercial and civic centre of Periklean Athens.

Iktinos, Mnesikles and Kallikrates, worked Pheidias and other sculptors, representing for example on the Parthenon frieze, that 'union of common aims and individual freedom . . . an order which never breaks down though constantly looking as if it would' which is 'a perfect illustration of the ideal of democracy . . . expressed in the funeral speech of Perikles' (Sir John Beazley).

This same Athens attracted to itself foreigners of genius, Herodotos of Halikarnassos, the inventor of history, philosophers like Protagoras of Abdera and Anaxagoras of Klazomenai, and they in turn inspired native Athenians to outdo them; Thucydides, whose narrative of the Peloponnesian War is one of the most penetrating pieces of political analysis ever written and, at the same time, a story full of compassion told with genius; and Sokrates, who turned philosophy, or at least one philosopher, Plato, for the first time towards the problems that have exercised it ever since.

In these fifty years, then, lies the essence of 'the Glory that was Greece'. But they were not all glory. The astonishing intellectual and artistic achievement is over-shadowed from time to time by vicious attacks on its finest products: Aristophanes was impeached; Pheidias, Anaxagoras and Thucydides all went into exile; Sokrates was condemned to death and executed. The building programme was at least in part made possible by tribute exacted from the member states of the Empire; the continued subjection of this Empire was an integral part of Perikles' vision of Athens' greatness. Worst of all, Perikles' policies led directly to war with Sparta and the other leading powers of mainland Greece in 431, a war which, for all his preparations, Athens lost, and which destroyed the vision utterly and beyond hope of recall.

There is nothing historians find it more difficult to forgive than failure. But an easy and comforting answer has lain ready to hand. Given those judgments passed on the Athenian *demos* by upper-class contemporaries or near contemporaries, like Thucydides or Plato, it was simple to find a scape-goat who was undoubtedly guilty at all times of some and sometimes of all the errors and crimes that had to be explained, a man, that is, whose faults were

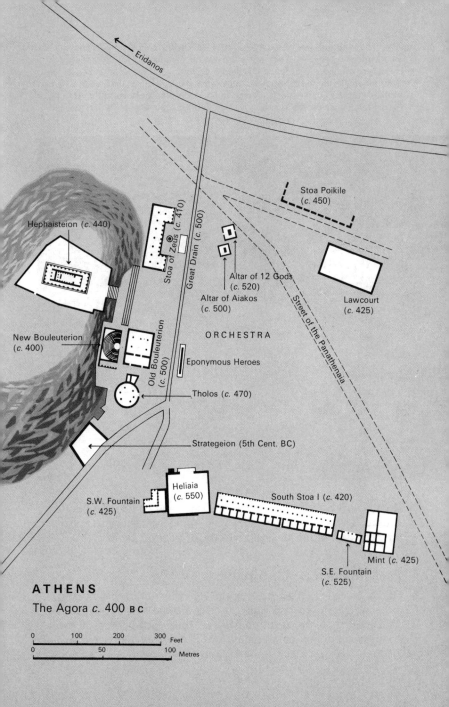

Eridanos

Hephaisteion (*c.* 440)

Stoa of Zeus (*c.* 470)

Great Drain (*c.* 500)

Stoa Poikile (*c.* 450)

Altar of 12 Gods (*c.* 520)

Altar of Aiakos (*c.* 500)

Lawcourt (*c.* 425)

New Bouleuterion (*c.* 400)

Old Bouleuterion (*c.* 500)

ORCHESTRA

Eponymous Heroes

Tholos (*c.* 470)

Street of the Panathenaia

Strategeion (5th Cent. BC)

Heliaia (*c.* 550)

South Stoa I (*c.* 420)

S.W. Fountain (*c.* 425)

S.E. Fountain (*c.* 525)

Mint (*c.* 425)

ATHENS

The Agora *c.* 400 BC

| 0 | 100 | 200 | 300 | Feet |
| 0 | | 50 | | 100 | Metres |

A model of the west side of the Agora (after Hellenistic re-modelling). The buildings are identified on page 15. The Tholos provided living quarters for the standing-committee of the Council (page 18), the Bouleuterion was the Council-house, the Metroon (replacing the old Bouleuterion) a public record-office, the Stoa of Zeus probably the site of an important court and of occasional meetings of the Areopagos (page 145). The temple of Hephaistos is a slightly older contemporary of the Parthenon.

already writ large in the ancient evidence and could be condemned without any sense of personal guilt (modern historians too have not been men of the lower-class) – the ordinary Athenian.

The Athenian Constitution

Guilty indeed he must have been. No constitution has ever given more weight to the decisions of the ordinary man than did the Athenian. This constitution was a direct democracy, in which policy, even in matters of detail, was decided by an assembly of all

The west side of the Agora today. The temple of
Hephaistos still stands almost entire. The circular
foundation (bottom left) is that of the Tholos, from
which, as a starting point, other foundations
can be identified by reference to the model
opposite and the plan on page 15.

adult male citizens; executive officers were appointed either by lot or by vote and their performance in office was carefully vetted by this same assembly. It met at a minimum forty times a year and as often besides as the chief executives thought fit. Proposals were introduced only by these executives or by members of the Council, but the assembly had full powers of debate, of amendment from the floor, and could even at times instruct the Council to introduce some specific proposal at a future meeting.

The Council itself, which was primarily responsible for formulating the Assembly's business and for a considerable part of the routine day-to-day administration, consisted of 500 members, chosen annually by lot from all parts of Attika, fifty from each of ten local tribes. No doubt many Athenians were unwilling to serve, no doubt anyone interested in politics could always get himself chosen, but no one acted as Councillor more than twice in his lifetime and the whole body must have been fairly representative of the citizen population, both economically and geographically. Then ten groups of tribal nominees took it in turn to act as standing committee for the Council, a committee which was in permanent session, living in the Council buildings, during its period of office, while a daily chairman, again chosen at random from the group, acted as president of the committee, Council or assembly as and when each was convened.

It is, of course, notoriously difficult to draw a firm line between administrative and policy-making decisions. In Athens, the chief magistrates, the board of ten *strategoi* (or generals), the only important board filled by direct election, must always have influenced and from time to time directed Athenian policy, even at the highest level, as a result both of the nature of their office, since military commanders must be allowed some freedom of decision, and of their personal prestige, since their election in the first place demanded considerable popularity. It was as *strategos*, regularly re-elected, that Perikles controlled the assembly during his supremacy. But, the *strategoi* apart (and even they were chosen, directed and judged on their performance by the assembly), no single Athenian

The temple of Poseidon at Sounion, the southernmost point of Attika. It was built to the design of an unknown architect *c.* 440 BC and is seen here from the west. Its brilliant white marble columns gave the returning sailor his first glimpse of Attika – 'Oh to be where the wooded, wave-washed cape stands out over the sea, beneath the level height of Sounion, so to greet sacred Athens.' (Sophokles, *Ajax*, *vv.* 1216–21).

or group of Athenians which was not a typical and more or less random cross-section of the whole community had a right to any significant say in the ordering of affairs without the assembly's approval. The only body which might have put a check on the assembly's independence, the Council, was itself an assembly in miniature, moved no doubt to act against it from time to time as a result of fuller information or more careful thought, but never by a basic difference of interest.

Similarly, decisions in the law-courts, decisions which might on occasion have momentous political implications, were reached by

juries of as many as 500 or 1,000 men who were again drawn indiscriminately from all who cared to present themselves for service. The professional speech-writer might have some effect on the vote through the quality of the arguments he produced for his client, but the presiding magistrate, the archon, who in any case owed his appointment to lot, not to any judicial expertise, had none at all. In origin the courts were committees of the assembly or the assembly itself sitting in a judicial capacity to hear appeals against a magistrate's personal judgment in a court of first instance, and when, in time, the court of first instance and the appeal court were, so to speak, combined, the archon brought with him to the new proceedings nothing of his earlier authority. Throughout their history the Athenian courts retained the essential characteristic that their judgments were amateur judgments which would probably have been confirmed by any poll of the whole citizen body.

A water-clock (*klepsydra*) used for timing and limiting speeches in the law-courts. The original on which this model is based probably belonged to the Council-house and carries the name of one of the ten tribes (cf. page 194) which in turn furnished the standing committee. The two crosses indicate the capacity and consequently the time allowed, in this case about six minutes.

Athenian society: the 'demos'

Thus Athens was run by ordinary Athenians. But who were these ordinary Athenians? When, where, and how did they go wrong? What were they guilty of? The answers have taken many different forms; some argue for a gradual degeneration of the *demos*, corrupted by power; others that its naturally gross appetites, held in check by Perikles, were let loose by his less scrupulous and less able, because less well-bred, successors; others other things. But all have in common that they distinguish sharply between the educated or 'respectable' few and the selfish mob, or between the squalid world of politics dominated by that greedy mob and the secluded world of the intellectual which Perikles, in some mysterious way, is made to share. That is to say that the ordinary Athenian becomes not an average Athenian, but something lower and much nastier, and his responsibility is limited to political decisions – and to the bad ones at that.

The demagogues who thought themselves qualified to take Perikles' place merely revealed the incapacity of a radical democracy to conduct a great war. (C. Hignett)

. . . the lower class which manned the fleet claimed the decisive voice in affairs and swept the state onwards [sc. to defeat]. (N. G. L. Hammond)

Flattery had now become the means of government with respect to that plebeian mass . . . whose demands already give a foretaste of the 'panem et circenses' of the Roman populace. (A. Bonnard)

These are typical judgments. The 'radical democracy', the 'lower class', the 'plebeian mass' can be distinguished from something less radical, less low, less plebeian. And who formed the lower class?

Athenians may conveniently be divided into oligarchs, moderates and radicals . . . roughly equivalent to the rich, the rural population and the urban proletariat . . . a classification also reflected in the military organisation . . . for the rich served as cavalry, the freehold farmers as the hoplites [the heavy-armed infantry] and the *thetes* [those who could not afford to provide themselves with armour] as marines or rowers in the fleet. (C. Hignett)

Now technically there is some truth in this. Since the days of Solon (594 BC) Athenians had been divided into four census classes, the *pentakosiomedimnoi*, men whose estates could produce 500 measures of grain or their equivalent per annum; the *hippeis* or cavalrymen, those who could afford to keep a horse and equip themselves for cavalry service; the *zeugitai* or hoplites, those fitted to arm themselves as infantrymen; and the *thetes*, those who could not. At first, as we shall see, these classes had an important political significance in that membership carried with it qualification for certain offices of state. In the fifth century this was still officially the case, at least to the extent that *thetes* were barred by law from the highest purely civil office, the archonship and only *pentakosio-medimnoi* were trusted with the chief financial posts. But even with the archonship it seems unlikely that the law was strictly enforced and, although lack of military experience, not to mention lack of armour, would effectively keep *thetes* out of the *strategia*, all other offices, as far as we know, were open to them if they wanted them.

It is conceivable, then, even likely, that when military questions were to the fore men cared to what class they belonged and be-. haved according to the military interests of their class. It would be natural too if some snob value was attached to membership of the higher groups. But snobbery by itself does not create political parties and the classes can only be identified with political group-ings if it can be shown either that military questions were always uppermost in Athenian minds (which they were not) or that the classes also corresponded with some other real economic, social or political distinction in the citizen body. The definition quoted above assumes that they do; *thetes* are an 'urban proletariat', hoplites are freehold farmers, and, if this is right, such economic separation might certainly lead to political clashes.

But is it right? Nothing is easier for us than to imagine an in-dustrial proletariat and to contrast it with what has almost become the modern historian's substitute for the noble savage – a sturdy peasantry tilling its sweet-smelling fields when out of armour. And, of course, there were many peasants in fifth-century Attika, some

An Attic red-figure bell *krater* (mixing bowl) of the
later fifth century by the Komaris painter showing
the interior of a small pottery. Note that the young
painter on the left holds the brush in his fist,
Japanese fashion. From the ceiling hang some
finished pots and what looks like a brush-case.

A sculptured frieze planned and partly executed by Pheidias ran all round the main cella of the Parthenon. It represented the procession at the four-yearly celebration of the Great Panathenaia (page 186) which marched along the Panathenaic way across the Agora and up to the Parthenon on the Akropolis. This section from the west side of the frieze shows young men preparing for the procession. On the left one puts on a wreath before mounting his horse; on the right a boy fastens his master's belt.

sturdy no doubt; there were also townsmen, though rather fewer in number. But the men who make up the urban proletariat known to us simply did not exist. Such factories as there were were manned by slaves, not by free labourers; there was not a single major job, domestic, industrial or agricultural, now performed by hired men which was not almost exclusively performed by slaves. The average Athenian was an independent property-owner, in the city an artisan, a trader, a shopkeeper or a manufacturer, in the country-town or village, an artisan, a shopkeeper or, more often, a farmer. Some were poor and worked alone; some were better off and employed a slave or slaves; almost all were independent. Nor is there any evidence to suggest, and it is indeed extremely unlikely, that there was any marked difference in the income range covered by the majority of the urban and the rural population. In short, there were hoplites in the town, *thetes* tilled the fields and, when the interests of town and country clashed, the political quarrel which resulted would divide *thetes* from *thetes*, hoplites from hoplites.

We can go further. A poor farmer or artisan today may see himself as something distinct from the successful farmer or artisan, may prefer to regard himself as a member of the 'working-class'. But in a society where no working-class in our sense existed, how could he separate himself? What would he attach himself to? Where, in fact, could a meaningful line be drawn in the ascending scale of prosperity? And if one were drawn, which I doubt, why should it be precisely or even roughly at the point which separated *thetes* from hoplites?

Athenian society, then, was much more homogeneous than our own. Distinctions existed, between noble and commoner, between rich and poor, between hoplites and *thetes*, between countryman and town-dweller and these distinctions mattered from time to time in politics as issues affecting different groups arose, but we have no reason whatsoever for assuming that any one permanent political group was defined by any one or any combination of these distinctions. We see the typical Athenian often enough in comedy or in the pages of the orators. He is by no means rich but he is not

An Attic red-figure cup of the early fifth century by the Foundry painter, showing the workshop of a sculptor in bronze who is shaping an unfinished figure on the right. On the left two assistants tend to the oven. On the floor and walls, various tools and 'spare-parts'.

a pauper: the chorus of Aristophanes' *Acharnians*, elderly country-men, charcoal-burners, hoplites and violently pro-war; Dikaiopolis in the same play, a countryman again and probably a hoplite, with at least one slave, but anti-war and thoroughly fed-up with all politics and politicians; the chorus of the *Wasps*, townsmen pro-bably, passionate democrats to a man, in their recollections of the past sometimes hoplites, sometimes *thetes*; the poor hoplites in a speech of Lysias who cannot afford their fare to Athens from an

A terra-cotta model of
a woman kneading dough.
From Kameiros in Rhodes;
mid-fifth century.

outlying part of Attika to attend the hoplite muster and their richer
hoplite neighbour Mantitheos who generously provides it (Speech
XVI, sect. 14). These men cannot be broken up into any neat and
tidy classes.

But two other arguments have been used to suggest that the
politically effective *demos* was not typical of the whole *demos*, that
political decisions at Athens might tend to follow a lower sectional,
rather than the national, interest.

First it is argued that those who lived in the farther parts of
Attika would play a much smaller part in political life than those
who lived in and around the city. They would take their turn, if
they wished, on the Council but, when attendance at the assembly
or in the courts might mean a journey of a dozen miles or more,
few would feel inclined to make the effort except when their own
vital interests were affected. This is certainly true, but it becomes
important only if we once more admit ideas of an idle urban mob
or, still worse, allow the modern conurbation of Athens and its
port, Peiraieus, so to distort our picture of the ancient city that
the mob becomes tainted with the smell and interests of the docks

An Athenian black-figure *pelike* of
the early fifth century by the Eucharides
painter showing a shoemaker
with a customer. Behind the shoemaker,
with no particular relevance,
stands a satyr.

so that we find ourselves talking of 'trading interests' or, yet again, of the *thetes*, 'the men who manned the fleet'.

But the urban mob did not exist and the men who manned the fleet did not live exclusively or even predominantly near the harbour. As for the traders, if they were not at sea and if they happened to be Athenian citizens (a substantial proportion of the trading community was foreign), they could indeed attend to public business – if they were prepared for a five-mile walk. For the Peiraieus was as far from the assembly-place on the Pnyx in Athens as half-a-dozen substantial agricultural villages.

Indeed let us get the physical facts straight. Attika was some forty miles long from north-west to south-east and at its broadest some twenty-five miles wide; estimates of its total population in the fifth century vary considerably while even the real population must have fluctuated a great deal with the extraordinary expansion before 431 and the disastrous casualties of war thereafter, but it is very unlikely that it exceeded 80,000 at any point (the figures here and in what follows are for adult male citizens). The city walls of Athens itself enclosed an area rather less than one square mile; from them ran other walls to secure communication with the sea and especially with the Peiraieus, again an area of about one square mile; but outside these obvious centres there were many other significant settlements, at Eleusis, for example, and Acharnai, which, so Thucydides says, could furnish no less than 3,000 hoplites, and elsewhere. Thucydides' figure must be exaggerated, but even if we halve it, even if we go on to believe that Acharnai was still by far the largest settlement outside Athens and, finally, assume that the 'urban' population spilled over well outside the city walls, it is not easy to believe that this 'urban' population numbered more than about 20,000 at the outside. Even if every one of these was of the lowest class (an absurd assumption) this is not a very impressive 'urban proletariat' nor a very effective one, outnumbered as it would be three to one by countrymen none of whom could have lived more than twenty-five miles from Athens and of whom perhaps half were within about ten miles. Ten miles is not far to walk when a vital issue is at stake. Indeed during the Peloponnesian War, when most of the worst decisions are supposed to have been taken, a large part of the rural population sheltered from Spartan invasion behind the city walls – did they not attend the assembly even then?

No, in war or peace there would be many small farmers queuing for their place on the Pnyx or in the law-courts hard on the heels of the city artisan and well in advance of the most energetic trader, and, given enough feeling, the rural vote could easily equal or exceed anything that the city could produce. In short the city did have a clear advantage in any normal circumstances; similarly the farmer from distant Marathon, the miner from Laurion, the fisherman or sailor of the east coast would be poorly represented, but there were other farmers, fishermen and sailors close enough at hand and the city itself was small enough to ensure that the geographical factor played no decisive part in determining the class-colour of Athenian political life.

Nor would the second factor which is often introduced – the existence of state-pay for public service in the magistracies, the Council and the courts. In theory this was designed to ensure that no Athenian should be barred by poverty from playing his part in public life. In practice, it is suggested, the prospect of financial reward for a day of idleness in the courts would attract the poorest among the citizens, the worst, the lowest, the laziest and most irresponsible. But, even if we admit that the poor are bad, low, lazy and irresponsible, it is still not clear that they would be the most readily attracted. For one thing the pay was not substantial, for jury service little more than a bare subsistence wage, welcome perhaps to the destitute, such few as there were, but not markedly so to anyone who could survive on the fruits of his labour, and surely less attractive to those who depended entirely on their own labour than to their slightly wealthier neighbours. If the one abandoned his stall or his vegetable patch for a day his customers would go elsewhere, the weeds grow higher; a richer man could leave a slave behind to hold his scales or his hoe and have a happy evening on his juror's fee before going home.

A scene from comedy on an Athenian black-figure amphora of the sixth century.
The chorus played a leading part in all comedy before the fourth century.
Sometimes they represented human beings (bellicose old hoplites in Aristophanes'
Acharnians), sometimes animals (the old jurymen appear as wasps in the *Wasps*).
In this scene they are apparently cavalrymen, recalling another play of
Aristophanes, the *Knights*.

Besides, we must set against the temptation of gain (and, of
course, it is tempting) a lack of interest in and aptitude for affairs.
The Athenians were probably more alive politically than any people
has been since but it would still be strange if the normal pattern of
political interest did not roughly repeat itself there. For one thing,
not everyone cares about politics and even fewer care enough or in
the right way to take action about them, particularly when things
are going well and when there are no fundamental political issues
in the air (and there were none in Athens between 462 and 411).

For another, action takes time and not everyone has the time to spare, not only the time spent in office but the far greater amount that must be devoted to all the other (unpaid) activities that a politician, even a humble politician must attend to. This is clear enough at the highest level; all Athens' leading politicians were rich men, not only because there still survived some old aristocratic prejudice, but because only the rich could afford to devote themselves entirely to the political game. *Mutatis mutandis* the same was no doubt true at every level. It would be absurd to argue that the existence of pay made no difference, but I doubt whether it did more than make the office-holders of Athens slightly more representative than they would otherwise have been of the population as a whole. It certainly did not admit a flood of the impoverished to positions of importance. Indeed, in advancing this argument, the modern historian simply echoes another error of the contemporary critics of democracy – the idea that personal profit was the only attraction the régime had to offer to the ordinary man (see below p. 229) – and he will often cite one of these critics, Aristophanes, to support him. In his *Wasps* of 422 BC Aristophanes sets on the stage a chorus of jurymen who do indeed make much of the lure of the few shillings that their jury service provided. But Aristophanes *was* a critic (who would guess from right-wing comment to-day that working men ever work hard or like their job?), but fortunately a critic with far too much honesty and sympathy to be able to hide the fact that for all their verbal greed these laughable old characters fought for their places on the bench largely for the sheer pleasure of the job. A farcical comedy is not the place to emphasise a sense of civic responsibility but everything comic which goes with such a sense of responsibility is there – the love of power, the self-importance, above all the pride of the little man who finds himself able to face and frighten the big. If we stop to picture the real men behind the caricature they are our own town-councillors, school-governors, trade-union officials, even jurymen, not ne'er-do-well scroungers who think of nothing but turning an idle penny.

To return to the point. The Athenian political system favoured those who lived in or near the city; it may have encouraged some who would not otherwise have engaged in politics to take an interest, but the 'plebeian mass', the greedy idle mob are still in fact the majority of the Athenian population, spread out among the poor and the comfortable, most of them independent, though very small, property- or business-owners, some oarsmen, some infantrymen, some countrymen, some townsmen, some old some young, some conservative some radical. Altogether a much less plausible subject for sentences which go on to ascribe to them one single aim, profit without effort at the expense of Athens' welfare as a whole. They themselves made up the whole.

Athenian society: the 'élite'

The intellectual or respectable few are no less of a mirage. They existed, of course, but not in any ivory tower. Athens was too small, far too small, and Athenian society still too near the days of aristocratic versatility to admit the existence of two cultures, of such specialisation. Aeschylos was first and foremost a tragedian, but his tragedies turn time and again to the moral issues raised by contemporary politics, sometimes directly to politics themselves. Sophokles, the most accomplished of the tragedians, was one of Athens' chief financial officers in 443–442, served as a general in 440–439 and was called in as a senior constitutional adviser in 411. Even Euripides, a man who was regarded as a recluse in his own day, was not above writing two violently patriotic propaganda plays in the early days of the Peloponnesian War. Like Sophokles, the his-, torian Thucydides served as a general and was exiled for his incompetence in the job. Even Sokrates fought in Athens' wars and held public office.

There is no doubt that the ordinary Athenian could be cruel, but nothing in the whole history of Athenian democracy could equal the cruelty, the blind monstrous stupidity of the few months in 411 and again in 404 when power was seized by the oligarchs, men

Fishermen on an Athenian
red-figure *pelike*, of
the second half of the
fifth century BC.

whose leaders, almost to a man, were the favoured pupils and inti-mate friends of the 'enlightened' philosophers; and Kritias, the worst of them all, had been loved by Sokrates.

The Athenian achievement

The distinction, then, is false. The élite was not untainted by the sordid world of politics, the mob was not a mob. Throughout the period with which we are concerned upper-class Athenians, some cultivated, some not, devised and executed Athenian policy, which was sometimes wise, sometimes foolish, sometimes noble and some-times wicked; throughout this same period the policies proposed were debated, accepted, modified or rejected by the mass of ordi-nary Athenians. They were not geniuses, they could at times be very stupid and very narrow-minded, but they were the men who listened to, voted for and presumably in some measure understood the 'lofty idealism' of a Periklean speech; who commissioned temples from Iktinos and statues from Pheidias; who gave the first prize in tragedy to Aeschylos and Sophokles and, with admirable discretion, the second so often to Euripides.

In short, whatever our judgment on fifth-century Athens may be, it must be delivered on all Athenians. There is no trace of any coherent protest against what was obviously bad on the part of any one enlightened group; there is no trace of consistent opposi-tion to what was good by the mass of ordinary men. All Athenians shared the optimism, the enthusiasm, curiosity, sense of adventure and love of experiment which characterises the artists and thinkers of the time; all Athenians were responsible for the development of the constitution in which they flourished and for the administration of the city from which they got their livelihood and their inspira-tion. All Athenians together committed one unforgiveable crime – they lost the Peloponnesian War.

Yet even this is not perhaps so serious as it seems now or seemed at the time. Like many other successful peoples, before and since, the Athenians had tried to do too much and failed, failed

The Erechtheion from the west (with the Parthenon in the background).
The area in front was consecrated to the most ancient cults
of Attika while the temple itself belonged to Athena
as guardian of the city and Erechtheus a legendary earthly
king. The unhappy olive-tree attempts to recall
Athena's own sacred olive which grew on or near the spot.

to make themselves masters of the whole of Greece, failed to export
their democratic ideal as widely as some, including Perikles, had
hoped. But it is worth remembering that for all their ambition they
did not start the war which ruined them. That was Sparta's doing.

In 433 BC Athens had answered an appeal from an important
naval power off the west coast of Greece, the island of Kerkyra, then
threatened with attack by Sparta's most powerful ally in the
Peloponnese, Kerkyra's own mother-city, Korinth. Korinthian
pressure, working on the jealousy that Sparta had felt ever since
Athens had taken over leadership of the anti-Persian alliance in 478

and on the fear that Athens was gradually overtaking her in power, influence and reputation as the leading state in Greece, soon persuaded even the less belligerent of the Spartans that war was justifiable and in 431 a Peloponnesian army under Spartan command crossed the Athenian frontier. As even the Spartans later admitted there could be no legal justification for this aggression. Not everyone would agree that they had absolutely no moral justification – would it have been right for the United States to attack Russia over Cuba or for Russia to bomb the States if, say, Rumania applied for membership of NATO? But it is at least certain that the vital decision, to make or not to make an alliance with Kerkyra, was not of Athens' seeking, and, once it had been thrust upon her, that she had virtually no alternative but to choose alliance. Given an awareness of Peloponnesian hostility (Sparta and her allies had come near to attacking her a few years earlier with even less reason on their side) she simply could not afford to let the large but hitherto neutral Kerkyran fleet be absorbed by Korinth. Perikles and the Athenian *demos* did not deliberately provoke the Peloponnesian War.

It is also worth remembering that alongside Athens' one dramatic failure must be set a solid record of achievement, not only the intellectual achievement mentioned above but the superficially less spectacular though in fact even more impressive political achievement. Democracy took a nasty knock in 404 but, after a brief period of oligarchy at the moment of Sparta's victory, democracy was re-established, and re-established with extraordinary calmness, moderation and good sense. It survived for another eighty years and during that period it provided, as it had since 462, peaceful, moderate, efficient and popular government for the largest and most complex state in Greece.

For fifty years it had also administered an Empire which included almost all the Greek cities of the Aegean and its coasts, of the Hellespont and Propontis, and along the southern coast of Asia Minor as far as the Gulf of Antalya; in all some three hundred states, a few of them, Chios, Lesbos and Aigina for example, not much smaller than Athens herself when the alliance was first formed. This Empire is often described as a savage and selfish tyranny. A tyranny it certainly was, if by tyranny we mean no more than the domination of one state by another. But, although Athenian enthusiasm may have led her occasionally to impose or at least encourage democracy when it was not wholly necessary and although at times she might pursue her own economic advantage at the allies' expense, interference in their internal affairs, political, military, judicial and economic was in general no more than was needed for an efficient ordering of the whole – nominally, and to a considerable extent in fact, the ally remained autonomous.

Savageness and selfishness are even less justifiable charges. There were cases of brutality, oppression and extortion but they were few and, while personal profit was undoubtedly one of the chief motives that prompted Athens to maintain her hold, it was not the only one nor was the profit excessive. The tribute which helped her to build her temples and maintain her fleet was no great price to pay for the external security against pirates and Persians which she guaranteed; at its wartime peak, nearly three times higher than it was in 431, the total was probably something less than could be raised by a 5 per cent tax on goods entering and leaving harbours with which tribute was then replaced; little enough when we remember that payment absolved the allies from the responsibility of maintaining a fleet on their own account.

If Athenian rule was as harsh and unpopular as it seemed to the deliberately 'realistic' Thucydides, it is curious how few of Athens' 'subjects' were anxious to exchange it for Spartan freedom – most of the allied contingents in Sicily preferred to face almost certain death beside the Athenians than to accept an offer of safety from the Syrakusans; curious that when revolts occurred they were nearly always the work of dissident oligarchs while the people were often prepared actively to support the return of the Athenians; even more curious how many former members of the Empire were ready to join a new Athenian Confederacy in the fourth century after less than thirty years' experience of Spartan freedom.

Part of the east side of the Parthenon frieze, representing the culmination of the Panathenaic procession – the presentation of the sacred robe (*peplos*) at the main door of the temple. On the right sits the god Hermes, one of a group of divine and supposedly invisible spectators; the other four figures are citizens or perhaps magistrates (the one on the farthest left has been thought to be Perikles).

That any outside rule should be thus tolerated, not to say welcomed, shows that it was on the whole light, benevolent, profitable and efficient and nothing could better illustrate the kind of service Athens could provide, the attention she was prepared to give, or remind us more vividly that all this was not the work of some high bureaucracy far removed from the day-to-day life of the mass of Athenians, than a series of decrees, passed in the early years of the war for the small city of Methone on the coast of the Thermaic Gulf. Methone had suffered some hardship and had failed to pay her tribute; she was also being harassed by her powerful neighbour, Macedon under its shifty king Perdikkas. The Athenians resolved (I summarise):

that the assembly should decide whether to reassess Methone's tribute or to be satisfied with a token payment.

that if Methone stayed loyal it should receive special treatment with regard to the arrears of tribute.

that an embassy be sent to ask Perdikkas not to interfere with Methone's trade or to march through her territory without permission.

that if the embassy fail to produce agreement, both parties should send envoys to Athens for further discussions.

that Methone should be allowed to import a certain amount of grain directly from the Black Sea and that the Athenian officials at the Hellespont should see to its safe passage.

that Methone should be exempt from any general Athenian decrees about the Empire unless mentioned specifically in them.

A footnote adds that on the first point the *demos* decided to accept a token payment.

One small example of the kind of problem, trivial or vital, which engaged Athenian attention forty times a year; the answers added up to a record that was good both at home and abroad and the man responsible for them was an ordinary man. Whatever his failures or his failings, he demonstrated for the first time in human history that ordinary men were capable of government, that democracy was not, as some contemporary critics said, an 'acknowledged folly'.

Most Greek cities of Asia Minor, Thrace and the Aegean joined the Delian League (page 207) in 478 BC. A few remained outside throughout, Thera and Krete, for example; others were coerced into joining, Aigina in 458, for example; others tried (and failed) to break away, Thasos, Naxos, Samos, Mytilene; Kypros had to be abandoned in 449 (page 13). And, throughout, the cities at the 'frontiers' came and went as Athenian ability to control them increased or decreased.

THRACE

BLACK SEA

MACEDON

• Epidamnos

• Apollonia

Byzantion

PROPONTIS

THASOS

Potidaia•

LEMNOS

• Sigeiom

KERKYRA

THESSALY

Pharai• • Pagasai

AEGEAN SEA

LESBOS

•Mytilene

LYDIA

• Ambrakia

Anaktorion

AITOLIA

EUBOIA

•Phokaia

LEUKAS

PHOKIS

CHIOS

• Kalydon

Delphi•

BOIOTIA

Chalkis

Thebes• •Eretria

ACHAIA

Sikyon• Megara•

•Kolophon

•Elis

Korinth•

ATHENS

Ephesos•

•Magnesia

Olympia•

Argos• •Epidauros

ANDROS

SAMOS

•Miletos

ARKADIA

LAKONIA

•Sparta

NAXOS

•Ialysos

RHODES

KARPATHOS

Kydonia•

KRETE

•Knossos

THE ATHENIAN EMPIRE ABOUT 450 BC

0   100   200
    Miles

0   100   200   300
    Kilometres

The theme of this book is the gradual development throughout Greece between 750 and 450 BC of the idea of individual human autonomy, of the idea that all members of a political society were free and equal, that everyone had the right to an equal say in determining the structure and the activities of his society. Athenian democracy was the result of a thoroughgoing application of this idea in practice, the most thorough we know of in the history of Greece, and, thanks to the peculiar conditions of life in a Greek city-state, it was possible for the Athenians to apply it in such a way that the individual was given greater direct responsibility, a more immediately obvious and, in some respects therefore, more real political equality than he has ever known elsewhere. The foregoing sketch has shown how the idea was applied; more importantly, though perhaps less relevantly to the historian's proper purpose, it has also shown, I hope, that the individual, at any level in society, can be capable of facing such responsibility and of exercising it soberly, sensibly, and with remarkable success.

2 Aristocratic society

The general pattern

Around 1200 BC the Mycenaean civilisation of Greece was virtually destroyed in a great upheaval of peoples which affected the whole of the eastern Mediterranean basin. Later Greeks remembered the local effects of this upheaval as the Dorian Invasion and, although their simple story of a more or less unified assault on Mycenaean power in the Peloponnese is false, there is no doubt that, by the end of the two centuries which followed the destruction of the Mycenaean cities, a new tribe of Greeks, the Dorians, had appeared in Greece or that their appearance followed a complete collapse of the existing order even in those centres which escaped physical damage, and introduced a further period of chaos, which, like the earlier, is to us almost entirely dark. All we know for certain is that by 800 BC a completely different pattern, ethnic, economic, social and political, had been established. Some few things survived, the Greek language for example, but in most important ways this was a totally fresh start.

Dorians and other invaders settled through the greater part of the Peloponnese, in Lakonia, Messenia, Elis, the Argolid and Korinthia; meanwhile refugees from the Peloponnese, from Attika and Central Greece and some enterprising Dorians crossed the Aegean to found new cities in the islands or on the coast of Asia Minor, often joining or replacing earlier Mycenaean foundations. This was no single, organised movement and, spread out as it must have been over a century or more, is itself sufficient evidence that sea traffic still went on; similarly cultural influences, as we can detect them in the surviving pottery, were communicated widely enough and quickly enough to confirm a certain amount of contact throughout the Aegean, but the whole complex interrelated economy of the Mycenaean world had dissolved and by and large each city, if it yet deserves the name, was self-contained, its only serious contacts, usually hostile, with its immediate neighbours.

In each of these communities political power was concentrated in the hands of a king surrounded by an often troublesome aristocracy or in those of aristocrats alone. This power was based, of course, on inherited wealth, wealth which at this stage existed only in land. Thus in every locality there would be a small group of large landowners, large that is by Greek standards (owning something between a hundred and two hundred acres); beneath them many smaller farmers who, with some landless labourers and a few artisans, made up the free 'citizen' population; some slaves, mostly female, house-bred or the prizes of war; between freeman and slave, in many parts, a substantial number of agricultural workers whom we might be tempted to call serfs, whose status would vary greatly from place to place and, even without variations, would be difficult to define. Indeed it is thoroughly misleading to use the word 'serf' which belongs to a world of very different relationships and it is simply cowardly to say 'what we might be tempted to call a serf', when we are dealing with a society in which it would not even be easy for us to define the difference between 'free' and 'unfree'.

In the first place it is misleading to use any terms which suggest too precise and explicit a formulation of the social and political organisation; it is misleading to be too precise because we lack the necessary information, misleading to be too explicit because the society itself while accepting or even creating complex socio-political distinctions, accepted them and created them in practice – it did not define them. In a sense there was a constitution, in that certain men and only certain men took decisions and these were accepted by everyone else. But those who decided did so because they did so, and most often because their fathers had done so; those who obeyed, obeyed because it would never have occurred to them to do otherwise. There was a legal code, in the sense that those who committed certain crimes probably tended on the whole to suffer comparable punishment, and those in similar positions tended to get away with or fail to get away with similar behaviour; but those who administered justice could not have written out a code (for a start there was no writing) nor could they even have recited it – they knew it in their bones. There were social distinctions of a precise and subtle kind and most men knew their station but

An unfinished sandstone relief of an armed warrior
with spear and shield wearing a crested Korinthian
helmet, probably late seventh century. It was found
near the shrine of Aphrodite in the sanctuary
to the Greek gods at Naukratis, an early
Greek settlement in Egypt (see page 162).

they showed their knowledge only in performance.

To take one example. To us it is natural to ask (and much discussion of early Greek history has been bedevilled by) the question: 'Who owned the land?' At the higher levels of society the question may have mattered and may have been answerable even then. But need it have been answerable for the poor? Many of those 'serfs' may well have had a plot of land that had been in the family for generations and would be handed on for generations more. But what is the test of ownership? Could they dispose of the land at will? Possibly yes, but no one ever tried. Could they be evicted by their lord and master? Probably yes, but again it rarely happened. The question of legal title just did not arise. Their title was like that of the aristocrat to the government of the state – it consisted in unquestioned possession, not in unquestionable right.

To use legal, constitutional, social or any other terms of a similar kind is, therefore, wrong unless we keep it firmly in mind that they are likely to have for us a significance which they did not have in the ninth or eighth century BC. It is particularly wrong to use any terms which suggest, like those which I used above, that we should think of this early society primarily in terms of horizontally drawn divisions, of classes. For, although it is clearly possible for us to impose some kinds of meaningful class distinctions on this rather shapeless world, they do little but divert our attention from the far more important vertical divisions of society which form the real basis of social and political life in any primitive aristocratic state.

These vertical divisions may be likened to pyramids. At the head of each stood an aristocrat; beneath him the members of his immediate family; beneath them a wider circle, the more distant relatives; beneath them again the members of the household, in the broadest possible sense of the word, free retainers, important or humble, and slaves. And the personal bond between low and high was all important. Such bonds exist today, between child and parent, between manager and board of directors, foreman and manager, labourer and foreman, but they are trivial. In early Greece they were vital and it was by the kind of link which existed between the man above and the man below, by the degree of loyalty, obedience, service or servitude which had to be observed, that status was determined.

In origin membership of a group would have depended on two factors, kinship and locality. At the centre was one aristocratic family and its estates. But in a chaotic world where virtually no state organisation existed, no family could stand alone. To maintain or improve his position, indeed to establish it in the first place, the aristocrat needed followers; at the other end of the scale the poor man needed protection, in the crudest physical sense, and looked to his more powerful neighbour to provide it. So, to everyone's advantage, the pyramids were built up.

As society grew more settled the need for a private troop of followers or for defence against a marauding enemy gradually disappeared, but new needs took their place; on the one hand the aristocrat needed support, labour, services and indeed material for exploitation; on the other the commoner had to have employment, assistance and a more sophisticated kind of protection, legal and political, not merely physical. But the relationship between the parties remained the same, may even have become more formal and more rigid as such things do. The private army at some point became a unit in the army of the state but it remained a separate unit and no doubt still felt more loyalty to its personal leader than to any national commander-in-chief (we may compare the army of the clans at Culloden).

Broadly speaking this kind of structure is found in every primitive aristocratic society but, of course, each differs widely in the detailed working of it, in the amount and kind of formal recognition it gives to the relationship between lord and servant, between the champion and the championed, differs, that is, in the kind of cement that holds the pyramid together. In Rome, for example, one powerful element survived throughout the Republic and into the Empire, the strictly defined bond between client and patron; in medieval Europe we can follow in some detail the working of a complete and all-embracing system, feudalism; the peculiar frontier conditions of early American society developed its own brand, particularly in the southern states; only recently an even more curious chance has produced a contemporary example in the Cosa Nostra of the American underworld. But the Greeks themselves grew out of all such foolishness well before the days of detailed history and we must not fill the gap by reading in to their private arrangements any precise details from other worlds. Yet for the essential nature of the system as a whole there is nowhere else for us to look.

The pattern in Greece

This as a warning prologue to the immediate problem – assuming, what is undoubtedly false, that we may even generalise about Greece, what special kind of cement bound the ordinary Greek of 800 BC to his aristocratic master?

The basic unit of the system was the family, in Greek an *oikia*, roughly a man, his children and his grandchildren – this at all levels in society, except the slave. Above the *oikia* was a larger unit, the *genos* or clan, a number of *oikiai* whose members considered themselves the descendants of a common ancestor. The common ancestor they accepted might well be mythical; if they were a grand enough *genos* he might even be a god, but this does not mean that there had not been a real ancestor of lesser stature. All members of a *genos* probably were, in some degree, related. Thus far no difficulties; both of these units are, in some sense, natural, their composition and structure readily understandable. But one of them, the *genos*, was officially recognised as part of the hierarchy of units which made up an early Greek state and it is by no means easy to see whether, and if so how, this recognition affected its natural character.

But first to complete the hierarchy. Above the *genos* came the phratry, still based in theory on kinship (the word means an association of *phratores* – 'brothers'), a group of *genê* now pretending to a relationship which it is hard to believe had ever existed in fact. Finally several phratries were combined to form a tribe, one of three in Dorian communities, one of four among the Ionians, except where some accident of history had led to the admission to the community of some additional group or groups.

At first sight the tribe, like the *genos*, would seem to be a natural unit, natural at least in the sense that it had existed for centuries before 800 BC. The same tribal names occur wherever we find Ionians or Dorians, and this shows clearly enough that the distinction had grown up before the Dorians arrived in Greece, before any of the Ionians had left it. But although in the days of later organised emigration the state would often prescribe that the colonists should be drawn from all the tribes in the mother-city, the chaotic wanderings of the first migrations could hardly have reproduced so neatly and so widely the social pattern of primitive tribal society, and we must suspect some element of artificial adjustment to explain it.

This suspicion may only reflect our ignorance of the migration world but there is another, stronger, reason to think that the social arrangements of the ninth century were something more than a natural consolidation of long-established gentilicial distinctions. This arises when we look at the bridge between tribe and *genos* – what was the origin of the phratry?

The word itself, like the tribal names, goes back to pre-migration days but it is used by Homer in the mid-eighth century (below, pages 62–3) in a way that suggests that it had played no part in the development of the story that Homer told; the references themselves are real enough and there is no reason to doubt that Homer himself gave one of his characters the words:

Draw up your men by tribes and phratries, Agamemnon, that phratry may stand by phratry, tribe by tribe. (*Iliad*, ii, 362–3)

But although Agamemnon is delighted by the advice – 'would that I had ten counsellors such as you' – the phratry is noticeably absent from the battles that follow; clearly it existed when Homer wrote, but it had not existed for long enough to be properly absorbed into the epic tradition which gave Homer his material. At some point between about 1000 and, roughly, 800 BC, nearer the later than the earlier date, I would imagine, an old word had been re-used to describe a new phenomenon. But if the phratry, as we later know it, is a creation of this period, it is natural to suppose that it corresponded with some real, contemporary, social entity and we think at once of the pyramids described above, one dominating family and its followers, poorer relations, lesser neighbours and retainers. That the phratry to some degree represented a formal recognition by the developing states of such bodies is, at the very least, a reasonable guess.

Thus all members of a phratry would belong at the start to one pyramid (at the start because we must allow for later shifts of loyalty). It does not follow that all members of a pyramid would be members of a phratry. Slaves certainly were not. Later, membership of a phratry was both a necessary and a sufficient condition for citizenship and although at this date the word citizenship itself is totally inapplicable, membership must already have carried with it a sense of belonging to the community in a way that a slave certainly, and perhaps others as well, did not. 'Perhaps others as well' – this is the heart of the problem and brings us back to the 'serfs' mentioned above. Was there generally if not universally in early Greece a class which was neither slave nor wholly free? And, if so, what privileges did it lack? Was one of them membership of a phratry?

There are two ways of approaching the question, through the classes and through the phratries. Depressed classes did exist, even in classical Greece, though, unfortunately, those we know most of, the helots of Sparta and the *apetairoi* of Krete are of little help. In both cases Dorian newcomers had imposed themselves on and reduced to 'serfdom' the existing populations. For them there was no question of 'belonging' (in Kretan terms the word '*apetairos*' in fact meant 'not a phratry-member'). Others, with one exception, are only names, the *penestai* (the 'poverty-stricken') of Thessaly, the *konipodes* (the 'dusty-feet') of Sikyon, the *gymnetes* (the half-clad) of Argos – the last two again are Dorian states. The exception is Athens. Here, in the seventh century a large class of small farmers was bound to the rich by something other than simple loyalty, tilling land which *de facto* belonged to the rich to whom they paid a fixed annual proportion of the crop and by whom they could be sold into slavery if they failed to pay. We shall consider these *hektemoroi*, 'sixth-parters', in detail later. For the moment it is enough to note that these men were Athenians but that they were not 'citizens' in any real sense of the word.

Again in the Athenian phratries there were at least two types of members, those known as *gennetai*, i.e. members of a *genos*; and *orgeones*, a word of unknown significance. There are two main alternative explanations of the distinction. Either, when the phratry was established, the clan or clans which composed it were also given official recognition as *genê*, so that those admitted later had to find a different name; or, and this I find a more natural answer, there were from the start some men, the nobler ones of course, to whom ancestry mattered, others with more pressing daily problems than a family tree. When the phratries were formed some were already conscious of membership of a *genos*, others lived no less in a family context (all men did) but in a more immediate and less self-conscious one; for them another title, a different kind of association.

But we are not much nearer a solution. There were in Athens (and, no doubt, elsewhere) men who could have been outside the phratry or could have been depressed members of it; there were in the phratries distinctions of some kind (*orgeones* represent the only one we know of but there might well have been others) which may together have embraced all classes of the non-slave population or may have marked only smaller differences, leaving the depressed outside. We do not know. My feeling is that every phratry from the first would be built around one leading aristocratic *genos*, that it would include another or other lesser *genê* and, beneath them, a *more or less* undifferentiated mass (I stress the qualification); that to be outside was to be a slave or, like the Spartan helots, a near-slave; that as ordinary men slowly won their freedom and those rights which were later to make up the idea of citizenship, they did so *within* the framework of the phratries which made up their state. But feeling is not history and it must be remembered that even if all this is true, let us say, of Athens, it need not be true of Korinth; even if it is true of one phratry in Athens it need not, in detail, be true of all.

However that may be, the general pattern is fairly clear. To some extent, I would say closely, the phratry merely reflected the existing social scheme, in turn, of course, confirming it and, when trouble began, helping it to survive. In war, law, religion and politics, the ordinary man was bound to an aristocratic master.

In battle only the wealthy mattered for only they could afford the equipment and the training needed; others followed behind to cheer, throw stones, even to fight with such weapons as they could muster, but only as supporters of the selected champions, each phratry grouped behind its leaders. The legal system, in so far as there was one, was entirely in the hands of the same class. They sat as judges and they alone 'knew' the rules which they had inherited from their fathers. It would be naïve to imagine that they did not sometimes invent them, if memory failed or interest encouraged. For advice and support all but the privileged few would have to turn to their own phratry leader – indeed in minor disputes between members of the same phratry judgment would be given at the phratry level without recourse to a higher court. Even the gods had to be approached through the same channels. State cults were controlled by hereditary priests drawn from the noble families; the binding cult of every phratry was probably centred at the home of and was certainly in the hands of the leading *genos* who again furnished the priests.

Finally, in politics, the leading *genos* provided the only kind of representative a man ever had. The political game was played in and around an aristocratic council which, with the king, if one existed, was the sole organ of government. Mass assemblies might be held occasionally to show approval or disapproval of vital decisions which could lead to disaster without mass support (a declaration of war for example), possibly in some cases to give formal assent to a choice of magistrate, but only to a choice that had already been made elsewhere. Popular reaction might affect the policy finally decided on but it could not be said that it in any sense directed it or decided it. The people met to boost morale, their own and the authorities' morale, to demonstrate solidarity, not to govern. The Council and the magistrates (who were themselves members of the Council or soon to become members) did that.

For the few men who mattered the game itself was a manipulation of the pyramids, or rather a manipulation of the other top people who automatically carried their pyramids with them. A common local interest might often bind neighbouring aristocrats (and their followers) together, or, of course, occasionally it might make them permanent rivals; a temporary agreement on some specific issue might be marked by a marriage which could, in turn, produce a lasting friendship. With a more or less stable agricultural economy and a more or less rigid social pattern, long-standing associations are encouraged; on the other hand, when everything depends on the personal decisions of a handful of men, small things can easily upset the balance, one man's strength or weakness, jealousy, ambition or even dyspepsia. There was always some room for manoeuvre, and the game was not without its interest, even if only a few could play.

In 800 BC, then, life for the ordinary man in Greece was narrow. He was almost certainly a farmer, with little or no prospect that he or his sons would ever leave the farm; not far from his farm, in a richer part of the valley was one large estate, one substantial house, and in it lived a man who controlled his life almost as absolutely as if he were a slave. This man was mayor, police-chief, magistrate, lawyer, draft-officer, commander, minister of religion, and a dozen other things rolled into one. Those not in his favour did not prosper long. And should the same farmer ever come into

A geometric jug of the early eighth century from Boiotia. The style lasted from about 900 to 700 BC and took its name from the bands of geometric patterns with which the painter increasingly filled the surface of his vase. This is a restrained example and gives considerable emphasis to the human and animal figures which become common during the eighth century.

A geometric neck-amphora of the second half of the eighth century
from Athens. The meanders, triangles, etc., are typical of the style,
as are the figured zones – warriors carrying the so-called Dipylon
shields around the neck; on the shoulder dogs chasing a hare; in the lower
band warriors again, some mounted in four-horse chariots.
These are *aristoi* – vase-painters were not interested in the *demos*.

A rhapsode (on an early fifth century
Athenian red-figure amphora by the Kleophrades
painter). The rhapsodes were professional performers
of the Homeric and other epic poems. One
group, in Chios, claimed direct descent
from Homer himself.

contact with the 'State' the same rich neighbour, with others like
him, appeared as judge, general, priest, magistrate or senator. We
cannot emphasise too much the complete gulf between these classes.
The few whose mastery was rooted, of course, in simple wealth but
had been so sanctified and strengthened by generations of command, so closely knitted into every aspect of the life of the community, that it now seemed to have been given by the gods – these
were the *aristoi*, the 'best men'. And on the other hand, the many,
of whatever level, schooled by centuries of obedience and by the
hard facts of life to an unthinking acceptance of whatever rules the
aristoi might impose – this was the *demos*, the people.

Hesiod and Homer

By a happy chance both sides have left a witness to their attitude,
both later in date than 800 BC both, for different reasons, old-
fashioned enough in their own day to be admirable witnesses.

Throughout Greek history the *demos*, in whatever sense the word
had from time to time, failed to produce a voice that has survived,
with this one exception. It is curious and fortunate that the exception should belong to a period where other evidence for its views is
so completely lacking. The voice is that of Hesiod, a farmer in the
large and rich agricultural area of Central Greece which later
became the state of Boiotia, an area whose economy remained
almost wholly agricultural long after less fertile districts, Korinth,
Aigina, Attika, had turned to other means, where ninth century
attitudes are likely to have survived well into the second half of the
eighth when Hesiod wrote.

His exact date is uncertain – it was probably nearer 700 than 750.
So, too, are the details of his life. His father was an immigrant from
Asia Minor who had farmed some rough hill land to the SW. of the
Boiotian plain. On his death Hesiod and his brother Perses divided
up the farm but Perses was not satisfied – he wanted more and was
prepared to go to law to get more. In the *Works and Days*, one of
his two surviving poems, Hesiod tries to stop him, to turn him from

an idle litigant into a diligent farmer. The result is a graphic account of the farmer's year, a calendar of drudgery ('work and let work follow work', 'strip to sow, strip to plough, strip to reap') and this not for riches but to avoid starvation ('wealth follows work' he says, but wealth is a comparative term and far closer to his thoughts is the advice 'work that you, with your wife and children, may not have to beg your bread from a neighbour'; *vv*. 212–3 and 382–400 *passim*). It is also a sermon on justice; on fair-play to Perses, on justice in a technical sense to those who administer it, the *basileis*, the Nobles.

No one could say that Hesiod was satisfied with these nobles; they are *dorophagoi*, 'gift-hungry', they are likened to the hawk who boasts over the captive nightingale:

> Good bird, why all this twittering?
> A stronger bird than you
> Has got you, singer though you be,
> And what he will he'll do.
> (*Works and Days*, 205–6; tr. H. T. Wade-Gery)

This is not the language of a man who loves his masters and it is often said that in Hesiod we have the first signs of protest against aristocratic rule as such. This is not impossible; the beginnings of a general discontent may well have lain in the eighth century, the factors which provoked it, as we shall see, were already at work and may have affected even backward Boiotia. But I am not sure how we distinguish from the poem between the private grudge of one man against a particular group of nobles and a general dissatisfaction with the system. Of the latter I see no certain sign. At the very least it must be emphasised that Hesiod sees no alternative, the nightingale does not answer back. The nobles may turn away from corruption to justice but if they do not, they do not – 'what they will, they'll do' (see *vv*. 213–85) – and Hesiod has no threat but the displeasure of the gods to hold over them.

But there is the displeasure of the gods, especially of Zeus for whom it is easy 'to make the strong and break them' whose

A Homeric-type singer performing
with a lyre – detail from
a late eighth-century geometric
jug from Athens. The scene
is probably funerary. The performance,
perhaps, in honour of the dead.

emissaries are abroad 'taking note of all these crooked judges who grind men down, forgetting that God sees', and here in the belief that there is such a thing as justice, over and above the individual decisions of the judges, and that there is some power which protects it, Hesiod may be voicing an idea nearer the spirit of the seventh than the ninth century. We must only remember that so long as men are prepared to leave such principles to divine protection they are far from thinking that they can act themselves.

Hesiod was not a poor man by contemporary standards – he writes of oxen and mules, labourers, servants and slaves – but whatever his exact position in the scale of wealth, he thinks and writes as a member of the *demos*; the *basileis* live in another world, in Homer's world. Like Hesiod, Homer was not himself a nobleman; like Hesiod he lived in the eighth century, probably rather earlier in the century, but on the other side of the Aegean in an Ionia which was already well ahead of Boiotia in absorbing the influences which ultimately broke the aristocracies. But his subject was not, like Hesiod's, rooted in the contemporary situation; it was the Trojan War, five centuries past when Homer wrote. His poems are his own but they are also the products of an oral epic tradition, older even than the war, constantly preserving but also constantly adapting language, form and matter, so that there is little in them of the eighth century except Homer's own genius, little, except the bare bones of the story, that belongs to the thirteenth. The social conditions, the attitudes, the institutions and much else besides are a conglomerate of the intervening centuries, a conglomerate that defies exact analysis.

We certainly cannot assume that the Homeric poems reflect in any substantial way the full development of the aristocratic state in Ionia, still less in Greece. As we have seen the phratry appears in Homer as an intrusion; the kind of social tie that matters in the poem is rather vaguer and more primitive, a man has his kin, of course, close and distant, and *hetairoi*, 'companions', those who follow or stand beside him in war, and are his associates or dependents in times of peace, altogether a less formal body than the *phratores.* Again the aristocratic household of the poems seems a much more autonomous unit than we can readily imagine in early eighth-century Ionia, the assembly of the Greek army before Troy behaves perhaps even more submissively than those that Homer himself would know. But for all that, kin and *hetairoi* make up a phratry-type association; the household structure may have altered with the development of a state organisation but it cannot have disappeared; an assembly still did what it was told.

Similarly, since the epic tradition was not only founded on the deeds of heroes but was created and maintained largely for the entertainment of would-be heroes, its outlook, its values were aristocratic, even more primitive, no doubt, than those of Hesiod's *basileis*, but not fundamentally different. Honour, above all, was what men strove for, honour among one's fellows and with posterity; honour to be gained by courage, by skill in war, in athletics, in the hunt; by pride which made a man conscious of his rightful place in society and determined at all costs to fulfil his obligations to others, superior and inferior, and in turn demand that they should fulfil theirs to him; by courtesy, generosity and even in some degree by wisdom. The perfect *basileus* was a splendid fellow, a loyal follower if you were his superior, a trustworthy and entertaining friend if you were his equal, kind, fair, tolerant to those below. He would accept a gift but would not seek it and, gift or no gift, would divide the estate equally between Hesiod and Perses if he thought their merit equal. But, in return, even the most perfect *basileus* expected nothing less than complete submission.

One Hesiod shows independence in the Greek army that sat before Troy; a certain Thersites, 'the ugliest man that had come to Ilium', stood up in the assembly and criticised King Agamemnon. At once Odysseus spoke: 'Thersites, this may be eloquence, but we have had enough of it. You drivelling fool, how dare you stand up to the kings? It is not for you, the meanest wretch of all that followed the Atreidae to Ilium, to hold forth with the kings' names on your tongue' . . . and as he finished Odysseus struck him on the back and shoulders with his staff. Thersites flinched and

A silver coin of Metapontion in S. Italy
of 550–470 BC showing the curious
west Greek habit of repeating the obverse
design on the reverse. The design itself,
ears of barley, advertises the particular agrarian
interest of this colony (see page 68).

burst into tears. . . . He sat down terrified while the rest of the
assembly had a hearty laugh. 'Good work,' cried one man . . . and
saying what they all were feeling '. . . I do not think that Thersites
will be in a hurry to come here again and sling insults at the kings.'
(*Iliad*, ii, 216–77)

Thersites, perhaps, was not a lovable man but he was not beaten
just for that. He was beaten because he did not know his place.
In convening this same assembly Odysseus had shown a much
more sensitive understanding. When he came upon anyone of
royal birth or high rank, he . . . made a courteous attempt to restrain him. 'I should not think it right,' he said, 'to threaten you, sir,
as I should a common man . . .' But when he found any man of
the *demos* giving tongue, he struck him with his sceptre and rated
him severely. 'You there,' he said, 'sit still and wait for orders from
your betters, you who are no warrior and a weakling, counting for
nothing in battle or debate.' (*Iliad*, ii, 188–202)

There could be no clearer statement of aristocratic principle.

A silver coin of the Boiotian League, minted at Thebes, the League's head, in the sixth century. The shield design may have been chosen because of its similarity to the Aiginetan 'turtle' – the earliest and one of the most popular Aegean coins. *Below:* A silver coin of Euboian Eretria belonging to the early fifth century. On the obverse, a cow; on the reverse, a cuttle-fish.

It was this principle which Greeks managed to destroy in the course of the next 350 years, or rather, not so much to destroy as to make irrelevant. The problem was not, that is to say, to bridge the gulf between aristocrat and *demos*, or, to put it more formally, to win privileges that other members of the community already had, to break in to the phratry organisation, for example. If I am right, most, if not all, except slaves or subject populations, were already members and there was nothing in the constitution of the phratry which could prevent it, in theory, from becoming part of a democratic state. Rather it was to create, virtually *ab initio*, the idea of a state composed of citizens who by virtue of their citizenship alone had certain unquestionable rights and to do this without allowing either existing prejudices or existing institutions to interfere in any way with the exercise of those rights, without creating or permitting new prejudices and new institutions which might curb or distort their development. In a word, to invent the notion of an autonomous human being and to apply it rigorously throughout all levels of society.

3 Economic expansion

Trade and colonisation

In Greek eyes aristocrats ruled because the gods had willed it so, because the gods had made them 'better' than their fellows. In fact, of course, they ruled because they owned and because their ancestors had owned more land, and it was a change in the economic pattern of Greek life that started the story of the decline.

Commerce of a sort had existed throughout the dark ages; the homogeneous development of protogeometric and early geometric pottery over the whole Aegean area in the tenth and ninth centuries, the spread of certain fabrics outside their place of origin, the occasional finds of imported goods, are proof enough. But it was a risky business to face the sea in a ninth-century (or any ancient) boat and the profits were neither large enough nor secure enough to tempt many from their fields. But more settled conditions meant safer, if only slightly safer, sailing, more stable markets, better goods; above all they brought an increase in the population which Greece itself, always a hard land for farmers, could not support. The scale began to tilt and more men ventured abroad.

In the eighth century ship designs become common on Athenian geometric vases. Even Hesiod can contemplate (with disfavour) the possibility of taking to the sea; as his father had done – and failed. Odysseus, in his wanderings, can be mistaken for (and despised as) 'some skipper of a merchant crew, who spends his life on a hulking tramp, worrying about his outward freight . . .' (*Odyssey*, viii, 161–4). Such men existed and not long after 800 some of them from the Euboian cities of Chalkis and Eretria established a small trading-post, Al Mina, on the Syrian coast at the mouth of the Orontes, where the chief caravan-route from Mesopotamia reached the sea. By 750 others from the same cities settled at Ischia and Kyme on the bay of Naples, others again may have begun to explore the southern shore of the Black Sea.

All this was the result of private enterprise, though no doubt the rulers in the cities took an interest in and even encouraged a movement that brought them Etrurian and Asiatic metal and

Part of a warship with steersman aboard on a fragment of an Attic geometric *krater* of the mid-eighth century. The galley is decked with lattice-type openings below for the oars.

manufactured luxuries from the Levant. They took an even more active interest when it was realised that new homes could be found overseas for the surplus population which the increasingly settled conditions of the preceding centuries had gradually produced. A generation or so after the first explorers the cities that were most short of land at home, Korinth, Megara, Chalkis, Eretria and others, began to despatch their unwanted citizens to found new cities, most in purely agricultural sites, a few in places of strategic or even commercial importance. But, although the motive behind the colonising movement was primarily a desire to relieve the population-pressure at home, its effects on the development of trade were none the less momentous. Surplus grain from the colonies found a hungry market in the mother cities who had primary products of their own, wine, say, or oil, and even manufactured goods such as vases to send in exchange. With the general increase in prosperity came an increasing demand for luxuries and for quality in everyday goods, and so increasing specialisation and still more trade, in Korinthian pots and perfume, Megarian cloth,

Crude toy model of a manned
warship of the seventh century.
Note the typical curved stern
and high bow with ramming
extension (a more sophisticated
example on page 70).

Euboian metal-work. By 700 BC perhaps a dozen states in Greece
had been transformed from virtually isolated and self-sufficient
agricultural communities into comparatively sophisticated organi-
sations in which, still against a solid agrarian background, both
government and individual had become aware that prosperity and
even survival depended on overseas connections, on the exchange
of goods outside the limits of the state itself.

It is easy to go too far, to imagine governments consciously concerned with such things as an export/import balance, with developing markets, with forming trade-leagues and the like, to think of
individuals becoming merchant princes, to talk about that 'new
class of wealthy traders' or manufacturers who have been credited
with so much in some books on early Greek history. This would be
very mistaken.

For one thing there was as yet no kind of economic theory even
of the most rudimentary kind – this is one field where Greeks never
advanced very far – and, without theory, theoretical thinking is
hard to come by. Greek governments did face economic problems

A mid-sixth century warship and merchantman
contrasted on an Attic black-figure cup. The
pirate vessel, an adaptation of the normal
fifty-oared galley of the time (a *pentekonter*),
is overtaking the large and elegant cargo-ship
which is innocently proceeding under shortened sail.

but they always faced them as immediate, isolated, practical problems, not as illustrations of any wider principles. Moreover, even
if such thinking had existed, Greek government never became complex enough or bureaucratic enough to be able to take the kind of
interest in commercial affairs that we take for granted. Thus when
Korinth needed more grain from Sicily, no one said 'We must
produce more pots', the government did not launch a five-year
plan for industry; no, more potters made more pots because the
merchants who brought the grain were prepared to take them in

Another illustration of a mid-sixth century
galley on an Athenian black-figure jar
(*hydria*) by an unidentified painter; the non-rowing
personnel are particularly clear – the bow-officer, ·
the officer in charge of the oarsmen,
and the helmsman.

exchange and, if there was a time-lag between demand and supply,
that was too bad – some Korinthians went hungry.

Again the wealthy individual merchant or manufacturer is
largely a myth; Kolaios of Samos, the first man to trade in southern
Spain (about 640 BC), became the equivalent of a millionaire on
the profits of one voyage, Sostratos of Aigina made even more – no
one, says Herodotos (iv, 152), 'could rival him' – but these were
exceptions. The ordinary trader crossed and re-crossed the seas,
buying and selling what he could; now doing well, now doing

The main burst of colonisation in Italy and Sicily began with Naxos (c. 735 BC); that in Chalkidike rather earlier; in N Africa about 630; after long activity around the Propontis (Byzantion c. 680), the Black Sea was fully opened up about 610 (Istros and Olbia); in the far west Massilia was founded c. 600. Chief colonisers were, in Chalkidike, Euboia (page 93); in Sicily and Italy, Korinth, Euboia and the cities

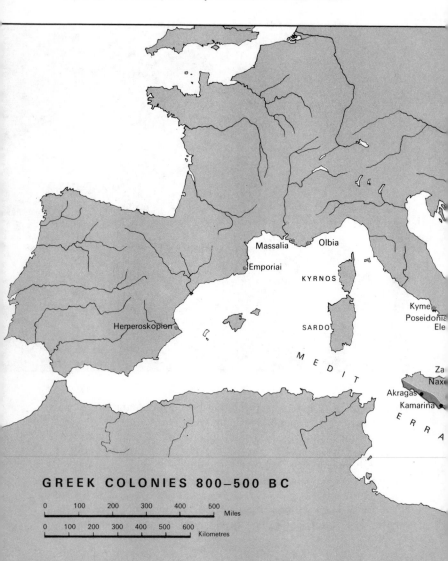

Massalia
Olbia
Emporiai
KYRNOS
Hemeroskopion
SARDO
Kyme
Poseidonia
Ele
M E D I T
Za
Nax
Akragas
Kamarina
E R R A

GREEK COLONIES 800–500 BC

0   100   200   300   400   500
Miles

0   100   200   300   400   500   600
Kilometres

of Achaia; in the Black Sea, Miletos and Megara; in Libya, Thera; in Egypt, Miletos and Chios; in the far west, Phokaia.

Oarsmen rowing a trireme, the classical type of Greek
warship, developed during the sixth century. The rowers
are ranged in three banks (only the oars of the lower bank
are here visible) thus allowing far greater power with
no increase in size. Crew (excluding marines) now
numbered up to about 170.

badly, losing all more often than he made a fortune. Similarly in
'industry'. By the fifth century there were substantial manufacturers, employing as many as fifty slaves, rich men by Greek standards. But even then they were the exception; the average potter,
carpenter, weaver or smith had a small family business, with at
most a slave or two to help him.

Both of these qualifications are important, but they affect only
the pattern of Greek trade, only the manner in which it might dis-
turb the existing society. They do not alter the fact that from 800
onwards goods were exchanged throughout the Greek world in
ever increasing quantities and that profits were made by someone

on this exchange. The effects of this development on society were complex and are now difficult to disentangle but effects there must have been – an entirely new element had been injected into Greek economy and such things do not happen without some disturbance.

Everyone was now better off, the landless labourer who could make a living at sea or in the city, or at least would find less competition for jobs in the fields; the potter whose wares fetched higher prices at the docks than they ever had in the Agora; the farmer, the Hesiod who, with Perses at sea, in a colony or serving as a mercenary soldier with some foreign king (another popular means of escape that widening horizons offered), this Hesiod who no longer had to share his father's fields and who might be growing in those fields some of the oil and wine that sold so well abroad; even the *basileus* whose vastly wider fields might earn him an easy fortune if used for the proper purpose, whose existing wealth, in any case, made it so much easier to take advantage of any new opportunities that offered.

But in a rapidly expanding economy, not everyone who begins at the same level expands together or to the same extent. Some labourers, some farmers, some potters and some *basileis* would outstrip their fellows or even their superiors, others could fall sadly short. It is here, in this shaking-up of existing society, in this new mobility, not in any simple clash of economic interests that we must find the real starting point of the political revolution. A lesser *basileus* who has made good will soon withdraw his allegiance from his old superior, if that superior can no longer back his authority with a larger retinue; a Hesiod or for that matter a Kolaios or a Sostratos who is rich enough to relax, to buy for his son the equipment and the training to make him a leading warrior or an athlete, will sooner or later begin to wonder why he is not a *basileus*. Unthinking acceptance of orders becomes questioning obedience and, at last, straight disobedience.

But all this takes time and would have taken even longer than it did in Greece had it not been for two other direct results of eighth-century expansion.

A reconstruction of eighth-century Smyrna. Smyrna was founded *c*. 1000 BC
by Aiolian refugees from mainland Greece (page 45). But colonists of
the eighth and seventh centuries still sought out sites of a very
similar type. A harbour, if possible closed, was essential; so too was a
defensible peninsula, well-watered and preferably of some height. More settled
conditions have here allowed the Smyrniots to move outside the walls.

Psychological independence

The first is psychological. The purely physical dispersion of the Greeks demanded more independence in the individual. The man who draws his boat down into the sea and sails it is no longer tied to the man who had previously ordered his life across the boundary of his fields. He cannot be, whether he likes it or not. He must decide for himself whether to sail east or west, what to buy and how much to pay for it. If he succeeds, he matters in the world and he knows that he has done it by himself. The potter who sells his vases by the docks must make what the foreigner wants, not what the *basileus* used to demand. The man who goes out to a colony may try to reproduce the kind of society he knew at home and may succeed in reproducing it, but he has to make a conscious effort to ask himself what that society was, and he has no built-in reverence for his new master. The mercenary must learn to take orders from any general set over him, not just from the commander of his phratry.

In these very different ways some Greeks were shaken free, willy-nilly, from their old habits; more positively, many of them were at the same time introduced to new and dazzling worlds which could not but fascinate, excite and provoke comparison with the poverty and backwardness they had left at home – the enormously wealthy kingdom of Phrygia which in the eighth and early seventh century controlled the Anatolian plateau (ruled over by Midas 'of the golden touch'); Phrygia's successor as mistress of hither Asia Minor, Lydia; the Phoenician cities of the Syrian coast and behind them the terrifying military empire of Assyria. Excavations at Gordion and Sardis, the capitals of Phrygia and Lydia, are still too recent to allow a proper assessment of the inter-relationship of Greek and Anatolian culture but it is clear that it was close; indeed the whole of Greek art was revolutionised by oriental influence about 700 BC whether received directly from the Levant or through Asia Minor. It would be strange if only artists were impressed by what they saw and, although there were no ready-made lessons in democracy to be learnt from the east or anywhere else, it is not impossible that some of the initial impetus towards political change was provided by eastern models, as it certainly was in mathematics, astronomy and a host of other things. At the very least many must have realised for the first time through these contacts not only that theirs was only one among many possible societies (that they could discover just as well among the tribes of Scythia or Sicily) but that other societies could prosper famously.

To take a very crude and simple example. Some time not long before the middle of the seventh century the poet Archilochos wrote 'Not for me the wealth of Gyges, I have no envy, I am not jealous of the works of the gods, nor do I desire a great tyranny.' (Fragment 25) – modest and unexceptionable sentiments, but with interesting implications. However remote the possibility may be, Archilochos can at least entertain the idea of a new form of government, what he calls 'tyranny'. He is not committed, as Homer and Hesiod were in their different ways, to the god-given rule of kings or nobles. More important, the tyranny he thinks of is almost certainly of foreign pattern.

About 680 BC Gyges, a retainer, presumably a noble retainer, of Kandaules the King of Lydia, killed the king and won both his queen and his kingdom. Almost all we know of Gyges and his descendants (who ruled Lydia till its annexation by the Persians in about 545), we know from Greek sources; for us the story of his accession, as told by Herodotos (i, 8–13), is a simple one of palace intrigue, not essentially different from the story of Agamemnon's murder at Mycenae and the rather more sordid and dramatically less successful usurpation of Aigisthos. On the face of it a Greek who knew his epic should not have been impressed by Gyges' performance. But there is something to suggest that Archilochos was impressed – the word 'tyranny' – *tyrannis*. It is likely that it is of eastern, perhaps even Lydian, origin; it is certain that Archilochos was the first to use it in Greek but not so certain, unfortunately, what he meant by it. Its history in later Greek was complicated. Fifth century poets could use it, apparently, as a synonym for

Another typical peninsular site, Emporio, a small port
in Chios. The harbour akropolis seen here was fortified in
prehistoric and again in late-Roman times. Seventh-century
Greeks preferred the hill from which this photograph was
taken and did not feel secure enough to abandon
it for the plain before the sixth century.

An Assyrian relief of the seventh
century from the northern palace
at Kuyunjik (Nineveh). The Assyrian
lion was one among the many motifs
which the Greeks borrowed from the
east (cf. figures on pages 84, 117 and 118).

basileus, king, with no hint of disapproval, but in fifth century political language it could hardly have been more abusive and we find the same overtones of condemnation in earlier poets, Solon and Theognis. It has been argued that an originally neutral word, a simple alternative for *basileus*, is more likely to have 'gone downhill' in prose and political verse (like that of Solon) while retaining its original meaning in more elevated poetic language, than a pejorative word to have 'climbed up' to respectability; that Archilochos, therefore, imported it for variety and no more. I do not find this altogether persuasive; it concerns itself too much with the moral, too little with the possible factual distinctions of meaning. For Solon 'tyranny' was already a bad thing – there had been 'tyrants' in plenty to justify the view – but we cannot be sure that a mid-seventh century Greek would have taken Solon's moral view. There was no reason why he should approve or disapprove of

Left. Statuette of a man on a camel found at Kameiros in Rhodes (seventh century). Rhodes was a natural gateway for the introduction of oriental influences to the Aegean and it even seems likely that Egyptian or Phoenician workmen were established there as early as 700 BC.

A pendant with the figure of a centaur – also from Kameiros, also seventh century. Orientalising Greek art is rich in monstrous figures of this kind (cf. figure on page 84).

the violent seizure of power, but there was every reason why he should want a new word to describe power taken in this way. Archilochos uses the word in a context where he is almost certainly thinking of Gyges whose rule was founded on revolution; the word was at once applied to Greeks who did the same; what Solon had in mind when he condemned 'tyranny' was primarily the idea that he might achieve it himself if he wished – again the idea of *seizing* power; Zeus, in Aeschylos' *Prometheus* (*vv.* 941–2), is called *tyrannos* – but he had overthrown his father by force; finally when Perikles calls the Athenian Empire a *tyrannis* he adds at once the explanation 'which it may have been wrong to *acquire*' (Thucydides, ii, 63). It would be easy for later Greeks to slip from the notion of the acquisition of power to that of the exercise of it; even easier for new moral ideas to add their colouring and their complications, but the word may long have retained something of what I would guess

Head of a griffin in bronze, from Samos, *c.* 600 BC. The griffin was another monstrous import from the east and in this shape became a very popular form of adornment in orientalising bronzework. A number of heads like this would be attached around the rim of a shield or a cauldron.

Right. A Korinthian jug (*oinochoe*) of the transitional period between protokorinthian (figure on page 107) and Korinthian proper (page 117) (i.e. 630–620 BC). This example shows how Korinthian potters took up and diversified the animal zones of geometric (pages 56 and 57), at the same time introducing oriental elements, e.g. the lions (cf. pages 117 and 118).

was an original descriptive force, the force which led Archilochos to borrow it (whatever its original meaning in the east), not just for variety but to describe a new phenomenon, a Gyges-type phenomenon, without any suggestion of approbation or condemnation. If so, he saw Gyges as a new phenomenon and, what is more, his words imply that he saw him as a phenomenon that could be reproduced elsewhere.

Whether Gyges was, in fact, different from Kandaules we do not know. At one point in his story Herodotos introduces an element which had played no part in the earlier tale of personal intrigue – 'the supporters of Gyges'. Gyges was not then a lone adventurer; he represented something or somebody. But what he represented is totally obscure, and I am not suggesting for a moment that early seventh century Lydia was in any way a parallel to, or served as a political model for, mid-seventh century Greece.

At the same time, however firmly a man might believe in a thirteenth-century scandal at Mycenae, he would be far more immediately impressed by a contemporary crisis in Asia Minor, and I would argue that experience of this crisis and of other eastern crises or even simply of other established political systems would help to prepare the Greek mind for changes at home, even if they did nothing at all to influence the nature of those changes when they came.

Thus far two points: that the separation of many Greeks from their aristocratic masters and the economic disturbance that resulted from it would weaken the ties between ruler and ruled and even cause friction among the rulers; that awareness of an experience in the outside world would introduce some flexibility in Greek thinking about these ties, would encourage Greeks to stand outside them and judge them as they could not have judged them before.

Archilochos, in fact, illustrates both aspects of the new psychological independence. He was born in the Aegean island of Paros around 700 BC, the son, perhaps illegitimate, of an aristocrat Telesikles who led the Parian colony to Thasos in the north Aegean. His life was spent in Paros, in Thasos and no doubt elsewhere around the Aegean, and his songs are of fighting and drinking ('By my spear I have barley-bread, by my spear Ismarian wine. And I drink reclining by my spear'), of hating ('I have one great trick; to answer the man who wrongs me with foul abuse'); of loving ('Desire robs me of breath; I am fastened through and through with the pain that the gods send'); of mocking ('Seven we laid by the heels; we are a thousand killers') (Fragments 2, 65, 84, 59). This is the first personal poetry and the first in non-epic form that has survived for us and it is easy, therefore, to exaggerate the novelty of Archilochos' achievement – men must have sung songs about themselves before 650. But I do not think that any would have sung songs quite like these. Archilochos was born an aristocrat and in many ways remained one ('Ignore the railing of common folk if you want to enjoy yourself') but he could mock the

A statuette of the late geometric period from Boiotia;
a two-horse chariot, charioteer and warrior. It seems very
unlikely that the chariot played any part in fighting, possible
that representations of them are merely inherited from the Bronze
Age tradition; but likely enough that they were still used by the wealthy
for transport – the smart young officer's sports car.

aristocratic code of honour (the singer has thrown away his shield
in battle 'but I got out alive. Why worry about the shield. To hell
with it; I'll get another just as good') (Fragment 6). He writes as a
Bluntschli not a Major Saranoff. More important than that, more
important even than his thoughts on Gyges, Archilochos does not
merely express personality in his verse (Hesiod, after all, had done
that), he flaunts it; he asserts individuality in a way that I believe
must be entirely new. Hesiod might well have said, had he been so

Projected drawing (by Piet de Jong) from an Attic geometric *oinochoe* (c. 700 BC). Again warriors on foot or in chariot (pages 57 and 87), armed with non-hoplite (Dipylon or other) shield, with two throwing spears (figure on right) and/or cut-and-thrust sword. The central figures here are thought to represent the twins Aktorione-Molione of *Iliad*, xi, 706 ff.

minded, that a swaggering general brought evil to his people; for Archilochos it is enough to say '*I* do not like . . .'

As a bastard and an emigré Archilochos, of course, would be something of a misfit in the aristocratic world; but for different reasons and in many different ways a large number of Greeks in the eighth and early seventh century had become misfits. They were discontented and no longer prepared to accept discontent with a grumble and a prayer to Zeus but ready to do something about it. What is more they had the power to do something about it.

Military developments

This power was given to them by the second result of eighth-century expansion – a transformation of Greek methods of fighting. Hitherto, as we have seen, a Greek army was a pretty sorry rabble. In the van an aristocratic élite, probably mounted for the approach to battle, for pursuit and, perhaps more important, for retreat, but fighting on foot with throwing spear and sword, protected chiefly by a shield gripped by one hand in the centre and strapped to the neck; equipment ill-suited to any cohesive fighting in the mass.

But there was no need of that; the mass could not afford to train or arm itself and rigged out as best it could, armed with whatever came to hand, it followed behind the experts to cheer and throw stones.

But even stones can hurt and a man cheers more enthusiastically if he feels that he has some protection against a wandering expert of the other side. So I think that we must imagine the first step towards change – this at some date in the eighth century – as a gradual strengthening of the defensive and offensive equipment of the ordinary man as he gradually became increasingly able to afford them, because of his own greater prosperity, because more trade brought more and cheaper metal into the market (above, pp. 67–8) and because contact with the outside world taught metal-workers new techniques. But the next and essential step in the development of the typical Greek army of the classical period cannot have been taken quite so haphazardly.

At some moment, somewhere, someone must have decided to use some of these better-clad skirmishers as a co-ordinated group, a phalanx of heavy-armed infantry, of what later Greeks called hoplites (literally 'armed men'), who, properly equipped and properly trained, could by sheer weight push their way through any number of opposing experts and, if brave and skilful enough could even resist a cavalry charge.

It is not easy to imagine the steps by which the change was made. The hoplite carried a thrusting not a throwing spear, largely useless if not flanked by other thrusting spears to left and right; he wore a circular shield, held not by one hand but with the whole left forearm, and this again gave full protection only in a hoplite line where each man's shield covered his neighbour's right side. At first sight, therefore, it seems necessary to postulate one sudden universal revolution – today the solo hero, tomorrow the hoplite in his phalanx – and many historians have written as if this was indeed the case. But how do such innovations arise? Does the innovator dream up a hoplite phalanx out of nothing or does he, at the other extreme, merely recognise the potential usefulness of something that has gradually come into being more or less by accident? Some element of decision is necessary; but where it came and how startling it was, we do not know. Perhaps the change came late and there were already many near-hoplites before there was a phalanx; perhaps it came early and first hoplite units formed only a very tiny proportion of the state's forces. But fortunately this is relatively unimportant. Any hoplite unit must always have included more than the few aristocratic champions, and in a mode of fighting where numbers were all important, the method must have spread rapidly both inside a state and among its potential victims across the frontier, the only limit being imposed by the economic resources of the citizenry who throughout Greek history were expected to equip themselves. More important than that; the tactical revolution is less relevant in itself than the economic revolution which made it possible in the first place or the revolution in equipment which the latter created and of which the former was a result.

Evidence for the date is scattered, slender and inconclusive. A few years ago it was thought that we could place the one sudden change fairly confidently in the early seventh century, but recent discoveries, a hoplite panoply from a tomb in Argos, a Euboian

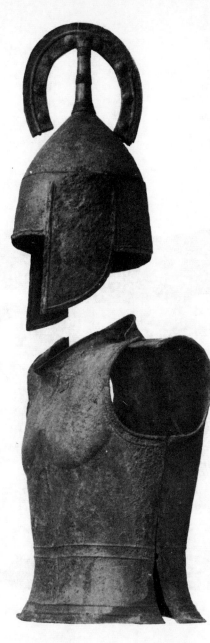

A hoplite panoply from a
tomb at Argos – late
eighth century BC. The
earliest preserved example
of heavy infantry armour.
Whether its owner was one
of many or one of the few
remains unclear. Again
some eastern influence can
be detected in the style of
the helmet.

The earliest substantial representation of the hoplite phalanx closing in battle, while (left-centre) a piper plays to keep them in step. On a very fine mid-seventh century protokorinthian *oinochoe*, the 'Chigi vase'.

vase depicting a mixture of hoplite and pre-hoplite fighters, suggest that the last quarter of the eighth is already likely to have seen the first, no doubt ill-ordered and unco-ordinated, steps towards what was to become the standard Greek battle-pattern. It is a likely context. Syrian, Italian and perhaps Pontic trade now provided the metal in sufficient quantities; in Syria Greeks could have seen new types of armour which could be copied, even new types of fighting which might spark off new ideas at home; above all, during these years the greater part of Greece was involved in a large-scale war which might well have provided the impetus towards and the testing-ground for new equipment and even new techniques.

This war, hazy though our notions of it are, is very much a part of the general development of Greece which we have been considering. It began, it would seem, as a local quarrel between those two Euboian cities Chalkis and Eretria, who had together opened up both the western and the eastern trade; before its end most of the major states on either side of the Aegean were involved as allies of one or the other, and although we are largely ignorant of its date (very roughly 735–700), of how it started, how and where it was fought, even of who won, its scale alone is enough to show how dramatically the Greek world had altered in the course of the preceding half-century or so, and to prove that international trade had already become an important factor in Greek politics. Two purely private squabbles between Chalkis and Eretria and, for example, Samos and Miletos on the other side of the Aegean could not have merged into one war in the ninth century nor could they have done so in the late eighth without some kind of glue to bind them, and colonisation, if we regard it as a purely agricultural operation, an attempt to get rid of surplus farmers at home, does not provide such glue. For home governments would not have cared where their emigrants went so long as they disappeared from sight, nor was there as yet any shortage of agricultural sites around the Mediterranean. Trade interests are the only alternative.

Phrygia had a strong hold on the route into the Black Sea and, at this date, close relations with some Greek states not only on the

Asiatic coast but on the mainland as well (King Midas sent a dedication to the rising oracle of Apollo at Delphi); in the Levant, Assyria under Sargon II (722–705) was pressing down on the Mediterranean coast and again became involved with Greeks (he was 'drawing Ionians like fish from the sea' and 'seven Kings of Ia' (Ionia perhaps) submitted to him). At the same time Phrygia and Assyria were at war in SE. Anatolia. It is easy to imagine how this eastern struggle might upset the existing pattern of Greek trade and lead to new tensions in the Aegean or more directly might set the friends of either power against each other.

This is no more than a guess but, in some way or other, it seems to me indisputable that the new economy of Greece was at the root of the trouble. It is at least certain that this new economy, to return to the point, provided the necessary conditions for the rise of the hoplite army (in a very loose sense), let us say for the first military adventures of a new middle-class, and it is very likely that elements of this army began to take shape in the course of this great war.

The effects of the change were momentous, if not immediate. The aristocrat was already losing his complete economic stranglehold on the community or was maintaining it only by exploiting the same new opportunities as his subjects, by entering a world in which only his wealth and not his ancestry could give him an initial advantage, where skill, courage, brains and luck were more important than a god in his family tree. Now at one stroke he lost his military superiority. In its final state a hoplite unit had officers but it had no star performers. The safety of the city depended on the combined toughness and efficiency of something like a third or more of its members, on some thousands rather than some hundreds of its citizens. Moreover when these thousands took the field they looked alike. They could distinguish themselves from and feel superior to the thousands more who could not afford hoplite status; they could distinguish themselves from the aristocrat who was their captain and from others who became part of the small cavalry force which some states maintained, but not from those who themselves joined the hoplite ranks – except perhaps by the brighter

A battle-scene from a Korinthian *krater* of the early sixth century. The warriors on the left give a good impression of the hoplite shield in use. With the figure on page 12 this is an example of the much more frequent representation of human figures in the ripe Korinthian (cf. figure on page 117) than in earlier styles.

polish on their shields. Farmer, artisan, trader and aristocrat stood side by side; and those who stood apart no longer mattered. And even at first, when numbers were fewer, far fewer, and the cohesion far less or even non-existent, the effects, if less striking and immediate, would be the same.

These would be twofold; to blur to some extent the old social distinctions; more important, to create a new sense of unity and common interest and a new feeling of importance among what

The fully-developed hoplite of the
fifth century. Notice the thrusting spear
and round hoplite-shield supported on
the left forearm. The vase is Attic
red-figure by the Achilles painter dating
from the third quarter of the century.

were, in the mass, fairly ordinary men. Members of a phratry had
looked forward to their champions; now, though still fighting as a
phratry they looked sideways, not only at their own *phratores*, but
along the line to others, dressed like themselves, drilled like themselves, perhaps, the idea would gradually dawn, with interests like
their own, and, after another look, with the power in their hands
to protect their interests.

4 Revolution in Korinth

The invention of political theory

In isolating these three elements in late eighth and early seventh-century society – economic, psychological and military – it is impossible not to exaggerate the immediacy of their impact, not to suggest that contemporary Greeks too must have seen at once their existence and their implications. But the bulk of new riches finds its way into the pockets of those who are already rich; psychological independence and class-consciousness are a long time in the growing, a very long time in a society which lacks the intellectual equipment for self-analysis. Before we follow up the effects of these new elements on the political development of Greece, it may be as well to show briefly how this intellectual equipment was at last provided, if only to emphasise the fact that as yet it did not exist.

The movement which led to the invention of mathematics, astronomy, geography and ultimately, history, logic, political theory and many other things began, as far as we can tell, in the Ionian city of Miletos, in the early sixth century BC. The new prosperity had provided the necessary condition of leisure; it also provided problems, in navigation, in architecture, in engineering, which demanded a practical solution but invited theoretical speculation; at the same time it supplied a mass of evidence, sailors' stories, buildings which stood or failed to stand at home and abroad, from which such speculation could start. Miletos itself was well placed to acquire from Lydia and through Lydia whatever there was of systematic thought in the further east; she had also played a leading part in the opening up of Egypt to Greek trade and Greek curiosity. But others were just as well placed and, as far as we can see, it was only chance that produced, in the early sixth century BC, a small group of Milesians with the energy, the independence, imagination, and, above all, the intellectual courage to begin this great adventure.

The details of the movement's achievements do not concern us, but it is vital to understand something of the methods it employed and to define the area it covered if we are not to be seriously misled

Head of a youth from Ionia (mid-sixth century).
In our preoccupation with the mainland
it is easy to forget that important
contributions were made in all areas of thought
and culture in all parts of the Greek world. Miletos
had both artists and philosophers.

in the history of Greek political theory. The Greek genius in the sphere of pure reason has not gone unnoticed. We all know that Greeks took over from the Egyptians their crude solutions of practical problems in geometry and turned them into the perfect deductive proofs of mathematics; that Thales, the earliest known Milesian scientist, thought and thought and thought until he persuaded himself that all things were made of water; that Anaximander introduced the notion of 'the infinite'. All this is true. But we sometimes forget that Pythagoras, greatest and most abstract of the early mathematicians, devoted much of his energy to explaining the very earthly harmonies of the lyre; that Archimedes rather later learnt a very important lesson in his bath; that Thales' preoccupation with water led him also to divert a river; that Anaximander forgot the infinite for long enough to draw a map of the finite world. If there is a difference between the early Greek thinker and the modern scientist it does not lie in his lack of concern for practical affairs or lack of belief in the importance of observation, though he did lack, of course, the resources and the equipment for the kind of systematic observation which is taken for granted today. It lies rather in a lack of inclination to check his hypothesis by experiment and to explore its implications for the future. Every scientific hypothesis implies the possibility of prediction and the Greek was fully aware of this; Thales was, no doubt, relieved and encouraged when the eclipse he had forecast for May 585 actually occurred; even more gratified when his anticipation of a bumper olive crop led to a corner in Milesian oil-presses and a substantial fortune; at a more serious level, Greek medicine could not have advanced as it did without an interest in prognostication. In other words the distinction I am trying to make must not be pressed and yet it remains true and important that, in his earlier years at least, the Greek scientist was very much more concerned to observe and explain the past and the present than to control the future.

Thus Anaximander (fl. c. 550), the greatest of the Milesians, collected such geographical information as he could and drew his map; Hekataios (c. 500) by further travel then wrote a detailed text including historical and ethnographic notes for Anaximander's map, and later collected and collated various myths and legends to produce a systematic mythology which, with the assumption of a certain number of generations between the days of gods and heroes and the present, became, either in his hands or another's, the basis for the first systematic chronology as well. Herodotos of Halikarnassos, also in Asia Minor (*c*. 485–425 BC), was led by the Milesians' example to record and explain another set of phenomena, the Persian Wars, and so invented history. These activities are less glamorous, perhaps, than the cosmological speculations of a Thales or the vision of the past and present universe which Anaximander created around his finite map, but they do help to remind us that, for all his boldness, the Ionian thinker always started from and often stayed close to what was given.

They are also important in that together they represent the nearest approach made by the Ionians to the systematic study of man in society. Anaximander explained man's creation by a rudimentary theory of evolution; doctors, like Alkmaion of Kroton (*c*. 500), already knew quite a lot about his aches and pains, but for both man was studied as part of the physical world which, in its various aspects, was from the start Ionia's chief preoccupation. But geography did produce ethnography; ethnography made possible the comparison of societies; comparison in turn encouraged a more self-conscious study of Greek society itself and of the variations in it.

By about 440 BC Herodotos could write an account of the respective merits of monarchy, oligarchy and democracy of which this is a sample:

Otanes' recommendation that we should give power to the people is not the best advice. For there is nothing more lacking in understanding, nothing more uncontrolled than the useless rabble. It would surely be insufferable to reject the insolent domination of a tyrant only to fall under the equally insolent domination of the reckless mob. At least the tyrant knows what he is about; the mob knows nothing. How can it when it is untaught and has no natural sense of what is right and rushes thoughtlessly into affairs like a river in winter flood? Let our enemies have democracies; but let us pick out a group of outstanding men and put the government in their hands. (iii, 81)

This is theorising of a sort but it is pretty simple stuff. Not much more than fifteen years later, however, a far less intelligent man than Herodotos, a man whose name is unknown but is widely called 'The Old Oligarch', could devote a whole essay to a theoretical analysis of Athenian democracy, an analysis which is often naïve and silly in itself but obviously reflects contemporary political philosophising of a highly subtle and sophisticated kind. On the one point raised by Herodotos he writes after arguing that the *demos* is entitled to power in proportion to its services to the state:

It may be argued that ordinary men should not be allowed to speak or give advice and that this right should be reserved for men of intellect and distinction. But the *demos* in fact is wise to let low-class characters speak. For if only the upper class did so it would produce good results for itself but not for ordinary men. As things are, when some low-class fellow gets to his feet, he lights upon a policy which is good for himself and others like him. But again it may be argued that such a man is incapable of devising a profitable policy. Perhaps, but the *demos* knows that even his stupidity and vulgarity, so long as it is combined with goodwill, will bring more profit in the end than all the aristocrats' nobility and wisdom, coupled as it is with hostility. Such practices may not produce an ideal city but they do preserve democracy and the *demos* is less attracted by the thought of slavery under an efficient régime, than by freedom and power. It can easily put up with inefficiency. Indeed what oligarchs regard as incompetence, the *demos* sees as a source of strength and freedom . . . (Ps. Xenophon, *The Athenian Constitution*, i, 6–8)

Herodotos and 'The Old Oligarch' seem almost to belong to different worlds and it is hard to believe that they were so close to each other in time. But the explanation certainly is that they stand, one near the beginning, the other towards the end of the quarter century in which political theory was invented.

There are two consequences of this. Like so much else in Greek speculation the theory was fashioned for a practical purpose or at any rate as part of a practical operation – the education of the would-be politician, a man whose chief interest lay in the present not the past. Again, like so much else, it was based on observation, and the study of history was not yet well enough advanced to make systematic observation of the past worth while. Thus it was a fifth-century tool devised for fifth-century use. Applied as it was at the time and by later Greek historians to sixth- or seventh-century contexts it was as inadequate to describe the kind of society with which we are concerned as contemporary democratic theory is to cope with the hybrid political structure of modern Africa or as Hellenistic categories were to describe the still primitively aristocratic constitution of second-century Rome (Polybios' desperate attempt to make them fit in Book vi of his History is a fine example). The wary modern historian tries to modify the terms or categories in consequence. But modification is not always enough; as often as not they must simply be scrapped – the word *demokratia*, democracy, did not have a different meaning before the Persian Wars; it did not exist.

Secondly, while it is difficult enough for us to imagine a society in which politicians operated according to a theory which is quite different from our own or for fifth-century theorists to imagine one different from theirs, it is still more difficult to come to grips with a society which existed without theory at all; yet this is what we have to try to do. Of course men were capable of basing political action on principle before 450 BC just as they were capable of clear thinking before the invention of formal logic or of measuring a field without the theorems of Pythagoras, but without any substantial body of comparative evidence, without any general theory of politics, without even the technical language that goes with it, it must have been impossible, except in the crudest way, either to produce a detailed analysis of existing society or to create in the imagination an ideal towards which existing society might be directed.

The causes of tyranny

If this is true, an apparently innocent, even self-evident judgment like 'tyranny in Greece was brought about by dissatisfaction with aristocratic rule' is false, and it is indeed false if we mean by it that men said to each other in the market-place 'I hate aristocratic rule' as they now might say 'I hate capitalism'. Rather they said 'I hate those men of families *a*, *b* or *c* who rule us', and their reason would not be 'because they are aristocrats' but 'because they have done *x* or have not done *y*'. In every state the men who were hated were different men and the reasons for the hatred were different reasons. Equally different were the politicians who took advantage of the hatred and the methods they used to exploit it.

Thus in Dorian Argos the kingship had survived with at least some of its original powers until about 675 BC, when, on the most plausible theory yet suggested, the reigning king, Pheidon, organised and became the hero of a hoplite army, with the result that he could reassert his control of the aristocracy and so earn Aristotle's puzzling judgment (*Politics*, 1310b26) that he was a king who became a tyrant. In Sikyon the tyrant Orthagoras came from the pre-Dorian section of the population and in the time of one of his successors, Kleisthenes (*c*. 600–*c*. 570 BC), there was marked racial feeling in the city between Dorian and non-Dorian. It is likely enough that this feeling had played some part in Orthagoras' rise to power. In the island of Lesbos, rather later, there was not one but a series of tyrannies, the result as much of factional disputes among the aristocrats themselves as of any popular feeling – or so it would seem from the contemporary evidence of one of the disputants, the poet Alkaios.

This being so any generalisation is dangerous and yet we must feel that a general explanation can be found for such a general phenomenon as the tyrant. Many attempts have been made to find one. For example it is tempting, and I believe ultimately correct, to link the tyrants with the economic expansion which preceded them, and it was once argued that the link might be very close, that the tyrants not only represented but were themselves members of a new industrial class, a view in itself improbable and certainly without any evidence to support it. Again, starting from the example of Sikyon it is possible to find or to guess at traces of racial squabbles in other Peloponnesian states as well and to generalise from these, but once more the evidence is lacking and, in any case, tyranny was not confined to the Peloponnese. More recently it has become fashionable, and rightly so, to insist on the importance of the new hoplite armies and to see the class which provided the recruits for these armies as the force which provoked the revolutions. That they were a force behind most if not all of the revolutions can hardly be doubted; that they, or they alone, provoked them, that the fight was a straight one between aristocrat and hoplite class, is less clear. Not only were there differences of much more than detail between state and state (the hoplites of Sparta, for example, had a totally different background from those of Korinth – the latter were farmers, artisans or merchants, the former farmers and only farmers; Sparta and Argos already had a king or kings, Korinth did not), but the hoplite class in general was not a simple and direct product of the earlier economic revolution nor were the effects of this revolution concentrated on only one part, the potentially hoplite part, of society.

But the only way to find an answer (in very general terms I have already hinted at mine – a growing sense of independence among ordinary men; an awareness of strength of a sort among the hoplites; a shift of power inside the aristocracy itself) is in a detailed study of the crises themselves. Lack of space and lack of evidence makes it impossible to consider them all, but in the two most fully documented, that in Sparta where tyranny was avoided and that of Korinth which led to the domination of Kypselos (657–625 BC) and his son and successor, Periander (625–585 BC), it may be possible to find some clue to the two basic problems; how much of the trouble in any one case may be accidental, may be peculiar to the state itself, how much part of a wider process and, secondly, what the nature of this wider process was, if indeed there was one.

The site of ancient Korinth. The centre of the city lay off the photograph to the left. Shown are the surviving columns of the mid-sixth century temple of Apollo and in the background the citadel, 'Akrokorinth', which was not only virtually impregnable in itself but perfectly sited to control the route south towards Argos and west towards Sikyon (see map on page 113). The surviving walls and structures on top are mainly medieval.

Aristocracy in Korinth

For nearly a hundred years before Kypselos' revolution in 657 BC Korinth had been ruled by something even narrower than the usual Greek aristocracy, by one aristocratic clan, the Bakchiads, who, we are told, passed the chief political office from hand to hand among themselves and were so exclusive that they would not even marry outside the clan. They had put an end to the monarchy at a time

A crude but fairly typical example of protokorinthian pottery (*c.* 680–650 BC) with the much-favoured animal-frieze round both body and lid. This type of box (known as a *pyxis*) was used for trinkets or cosmetics. (Cf. figures on pages 85 and 92.)

when Korinth, with its particularly restricted territory, had already begun to exploit its admirable situation at the crossroads of the east–west sea-routes through the Saronic and the Korinthian gulfs and the north–south land route from central Greece to the Peloponnese (a Korinthian settlement had been established in Ithaka to the west around 800; Korinthian ware of about 750 has been found at Al Mina in the east) and it is tempting to imagine that the Bakchiads may have owed something of their special authority over their aristocratic fellows to an especially early appreciation of the new opportunities. At any rate, once in power, they did not stand aloof from them. Korinth's two great colonies in the west, Syrakuse and Kerkyra (both 734 BC), the second certainly in part a commercial venture, were led out by members of the clan; another member, the poet Eumelos, showed an interest in the Black Sea area; they became involved in the international and I have argued commercial Lelantine war and their rule is summed up by Strabo in the words 'they took unrestrained toll of the market' (p. 378).

Strabo *need* not mean more by this than that they grew fat on harbour dues; the colonies *may* have seemed to them no more than an outlet for the domestic embarrassment of surplus population (though I do not believe that they did); they *may* have been dragged into the war by hatred of their neighbours, the Megarians, and nothing else; the brilliant adaptation of oriental designs and the consequent creation of what we call protokorinthian pottery, a fine ware which won a near monopoly of Mediterranean markets from about 700 BC onwards, was the achievement of numberless Korinthian potters, not the deliberate policy of Korinthian government; the spread of this ware and of other Korinthian products to Etruria, Syria and even the wilds of Macedonia was due to the enterprise of Korinthian and other small 'tramp' captains. Even so I find it impossible to believe that the extraordinary flowering of Korinth between 750 and 650 went on in spite of the Bakchiads. It must have had their active encouragement.

In this respect, then, the example of Korinth clearly tells against any simple form of the view that the revolution, when it came, was due to a direct clash of basic economic interest, potters against land owners for example. Bakchiads eagerly followed, if they did not lead, the trend to commerce. Nor is there any evidence as is sometimes suggested that they followed, or led, with any less competence towards the end of their rule, that it was the result of a modified economic clash, energetic merchants against less energetic ones. At the end of the Lelantine War, about 700, a Megarian tombstone tells us, Korinth was driven out of some border land she had previously seized from Megara but, even if this was a disaster at the time, it happened a good thirty years before the Bakchiads were expelled. Much nearer in time, there was, says Thucydides, a sea-battle between Korinth and her colony Kerkyra, 260 years before the end of the Peloponnesian War, i.e. in 664. But there is reason to think that Thucydides calculated this date not by years but in generations of forty years (the bane of early Greek chronography) and that 260 therefore means $6\frac{1}{2}$ of these generations, in fact about 210–220 years. Besides, even if his date is right, we do not know who won the battle. A colony was always independent of its mother-city and it could be that Kerkyra was trying to resist (unsuccessfully) some further Korinthian expansion in the Adriatic. Finally, it is argued, the growing power of Argos under King Pheidon (p. 104) must have caused trouble for neighbouring Korinth. Indeed it must but in one of two surviving stories which connect Pheidon with Korinthian affairs an Argive plot is foiled by an informer, in the other Pheidon himself is killed while trying to interfere. I shall suggest shortly that Pheidon did help to destroy Bakchiad rule, though dying in the attempt, but we have no positive reason to assert that in their handling of Korinth's affairs, external or internal, the Bakchiads towards the end were losing their grip, that they were not in 658 the same competent, adventurous, expansionist leaders that we like to think they were in the previous century. Archaeology tells us nothing but a story of steady and unbroken economic growth and in this case archaeology may not be lying.

This is not to say that the Bakchiads were competent; still less that Korinthians thought them competent; only that incompetence is neither recorded nor proven and that if the charge was made, as it doubtless was, it is as likely to be the result of some other, deeper, discontent, as the real motive for their expulsion.

The sources do preserve other charges. The story of Kypselos' rise to power is told in detail by two ancient authors, Herodotos (v. 92) and, indirectly, by Ephoros, a fourth-century historian of vast industry, learning and popularity but little discrimination.

Apart from them we have only scraps of detail, usually unverifiable. Much of Herodotos' account is fairy-tale, much of the rest of it distorted by its context (it is told as part of a general argument against tyranny of which Kypselos is held up, not very successfully, as a black example); in Ephoros the fairy-tale element is dropped and there is no obvious attempt to distort in any particular interest but one cannot but suspect that at least some of the circumstantial detail was dreamed up by the rationalising Ephoros to fill the resultant gaps and produce a 'realistic' story. But the outline is common and both it and even some of the details are likely to be true.

Kypselos, it is agreed, was the son of a non-Bakchiad, indeed non-Dorian, father Aëtion and a Bakchiad mother, Labda, whose lameness had persuaded the clan to break its normal rule of intermarriage. When the child was born they regretted their decision and tried to kill him; but Kypselos escaped and after a period of exile (this is explicit only in Ephoros but is reasonable enough) returned to Korinth where, with the support of Apollo's oracle at Delphi, he seized power, expelling some Bakchiads and killing others. Ephoros then asserts, and Herodotos cannot entirely conceal, that Kypselos was a mild, popular and efficient ruler – 'he had no bodyguard'.

Neither in this nor in the other, scrappier sources is there any hint of Bakchiad incompetence, except in their sad failure to exterminate the future tyrant. Rather they are cruel, suspicious, arbitrary and exclusive. Now cruelty and suspicion are common enough in any ruler or ruling class which finds its position threatened and, whether they exist or not, are likely to be discerned by those who threaten it. In any case they, like incompetence, are or may be purely personal, i.e. accidental, failings in a régime; with arbitrariness and exclusiveness we move nearer to something that concerns a régime as such (exclusiveness at least belongs to an aristocracy by definition), and if these were really felt by Korinthians in 657 it might mean the beginnings of dissatisfaction with aristocracy *qua* aristocracy.

Happily there is some reason to believe that they felt both. Neither Herodotos nor Ephoros could be trusted on a point like

this; neither is proof against anachronism. But Herodotos has preserved, as a decoration to his tale, a number of Delphic oracles, two of which are certainly contemporary or very nearly contemporary with the revolution. One of them, said to have encouraged Kypselos to make his attempt, forecasts the duration of the tyranny (this presumably a later addition) and describes Kypselos himself as 'King of famous Korinth'. If this was indeed delivered to him while the Bakchiads still reigned, as Herodotos says and I am inclined to believe, then Delphi was offering him both encouragement and credentials to present to the people of Korinth. The other is addressed to his father Aëtion, in theory before Kypselos' birth, and foretells, rather too accurately, the boy's later achievements.

Aëtion, no one honours you though you deserve great honour. Labda is with child and will bear a rock which will roll down upon those who rule alone, and will set Korinth to rights.

No one will believe that these words were said to Aëtion. But I am sure that they were invented at the time of Kypselos' own consultation, or, at the latest, very soon after his success. Delphi would not have drawn attention to the singleness of Bakchiad rule when Kypselos himself was fully established in an even more exclusive position. They are good evidence then for the Delphic attitude to the Bakchiads at the time and, if they were to serve any purpose as propaganda for Kypselos, for the Korinthian attitude as well.

The Bakchiads, then, were thought of as 'men who ruled alone' (*mounarchoi*), and under them Korinth needed to be 'set to rights': Kypselos *dikaiosei Korinthon*. It is not easy to get the exact sense. The adjective *dikaios*, from which the verb is formed, meant in later Greek very much the same as 'just' but earlier, in Homer for example, it has much less of a moral flavour, not 'living in accordance with the laws of god or man' (tacitly assumed to be right) but rather 'living according to some rule'; its opposite not 'unjust' or 'impious' but 'wild, uncivilised'. We cannot be certain but it is this earlier sense that I feel here.

To the SE Korinthian territory marched with Argos, to the NE with Megara, to the W with Sikyon, but she showed little ambition for domestic expansion and was normally content to exploit her control of the sea and land crossroads, a control which went more or less unchallenged until in the fifth century Athens took over the Saronic Gulf from Aigina and even established a hold on the Korinthian Gulf at Naupaktos.

On this contemporary evidence, then, some Korinthians were arguing that power should be more widely shared and some that Korinth needed, what Hesiod had longed for without much hope in eighth-century Boiotia, better justice, or more precisely some set of rules in place of Bakchiad arbitrariness.

The hoplites and Kypselos

In moving on to ask the essential question, who wanted what, it is as well to admit at the start that we are largely guessing. There is no seventh-century Hesiod. Had one existed he would have been a substantial hoplite; but how far would this substantial hoplite have moved from Hesiod's grumbling but negative dislike of his wicked *basileis*? We simply do not know. That he had taken one great step is clear enough; his dislike was no longer negative. He had come or he had been brought to see that if a government was disliked, it could be changed and he was confident enough to give his help in changing it. This because there can be no doubt at all that the hoplites of Korinth backed Kypselos.

According to Ephoros Kypselos held military office after his return from exile and before his *coup*, but although this is probable enough in itself and would give him a fine chance to win the army's favour, it could equally well be drawn from Ephoros' imagination as from any genuine tradition. Less likely to be false is the claim that he never had a bodyguard – again a fair pointer to army support. But, in any case, we hardly need evidence – Kypselos won; he could not have defeated the Bakchiads against the army's opposition, he could hardly have done it without their enthusiastic co-operation.

To have realised that change was possible, that Zeus had not confirmed the *basileis* in power for ever, that ordinary men could take a hand in choosing the government they would have, all this is a momentous advance. But why did the hoplites want a change? Did they want anything more than the material benefits which would come, they thought, from efficient and sympathetic govern-

It is less easy to say whether he was interested in justice. Hesiod had felt the lack of it; to provide it as we shall see was one of the chief preoccupations of all seventh-century reformers. The desire for it can be detected in the oracle; unlike political power it is the kind of thing an ordinary man might be prepared to fight for. All we lack is good evidence that he did fight for it or that Kypselos was concerned to give it to him.

Doubtful evidence there is. Ephoros, it will be remembered, credited Kypselos with military office under the Bakchiads. In that office, he goes on, Kypselos won popularity by his lenient administration of the law governing debtors. There is nothing odd in this combination of military and civil functions; the aristocratic magistrate, however much of an amateur in all fields, was always regarded as omni-competent and as late as 490 a man of no qualifications except his birth and wealth was called away from the court over which he normally presided to command the Athenian army at Marathon. Indeed it is almost an argument in favour of the tale – Ephoros himself lived in days of greater professionalism. But a doubt remains, and even if it did not, decency about debt is not quite the same thing as the creation of a new law code. We must say more of justice later; for the moment let us return to the question of power.

Kypselos' party

Someone in Korinth wanted it. Kypselos, obviously. But Kypselos however authoritarian, did not rule alone. So long as we are prepared to entertain vague thoughts about the pretentions of the hoplites, they, as a mass, can fill in the background, but, if politically minded hoplites are a mirage, as they are, others must be found. We do not need to look far. Without the support of a fair proportion of the available, that is the already trained, administrative talent a revolution either fails altogether or succeeds only after a period of confusion (and this is true even of an uncomplicated state like seventh-century Korinth); there is no evidence

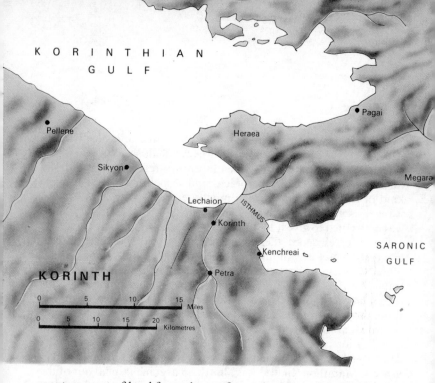

ment, a grant of land from the confiscated estates of the aristocrats, lower taxes or the like? Perhaps not.

At least it is certain that they did not want a share of political power, though it is often loosely claimed that they did. True, to overthrow one government and establish a new one is, in a sense, to exercise political power, but not in any normal sense, and it is perhaps an illustration of the Korinthian hoplites' still only half-developed feeling of independence that the man they were prepared to follow against the Bakchiads was himself almost a Bakchiad. Though hating Bakchiads it is as if they still felt happier behind a Bakchiad. But the conclusive proof that they had no desire as yet for a voice in government is that although their hero Kypselos did not give them one, he still, as far as we can see, remained their hero. Nearly a century after his accession the tyranny fell and even then the hoplite was left out of any significant role in politics; Korinth became, and for about 200 years remained a narrow oligarchy. A politically conscious and ambitious *demos* could hardly have been restrained for so long.

whatsoever that Kypselos brought anything but immediate and continuous success. It follows that he could call on men who already knew how to govern, to command an army, sit in a court, administer a market. An ordinary hoplite knew none of these things.

Kypselos, as a fringe-member of the ruling clan did. There must have been other fringe-members – intermarriage does not prevent the appearance of an occasional Archilochos; and, more important, there must have been members of other clans, who after the economic shake-up of the preceding century had found themselves the equals of the Bakchiads in everything except political recognition. They had always ruled their own phratries, in war, in peace, in politics, in religion and in the courts; now, by all the rules of aristocratic government, they should have a chance to share the rule of the state as well, but they were denied it by the Bakchiad monopoly. There came a moment when they were prepared to fight and in order to fight they did two things, one fatal for their fame, the other fatal for their future; since revolution by committee is never easy they fought not for themselves but for Kypselos as their champion, and since revolution without the army was no longer possible they enlisted the support of the hoplites, of the men who, in time, even in right-minded Korinth, would see to it that their claims to individual distinction were forgotten.

This is not to say that they immediately regretted their mistake. Just as subservience to the Princeps was a small price to pay for the domination that the great revolutionary families of Italy won in Augustan Rome, so, I would imagine, the nameless powerful supporters of Kypselos rejoiced in their new authority and willingly did the necessary obeisance, and, since Kypselos could hardly have been such a prig as Augustus, the obeisance may not have needed to be very deep. But the Roman parallel also holds for Kypselos' son and successor Periander, and with his reign comes further confirmation if it were needed, of the existence of these important men. Augustus' heir, Tiberius, has a bad record, partly due to his own character, but partly, also, to the envy of those who, at Augustus' death, felt that they were equally fit to fill his place. A second generation despot has no right to his father's place. He must either abdicate, like Richard Cromwell, or resist with force, like Tiberius or Periander. In either case he abdicates in the face of, or offers resistance to the same men, those who have stood closest to power in his father's day. Periander, the story goes, was given good advice on how to maintain his tyranny – 'lop off the tallest ears of corn'. Note that it is the tallest, the men who had stood behind Kypselos' throne. And, when the tyranny in Korinth finally fell, a Council of Eighty took office. I should not be surprised if more than half of those eighty had grandfathers whom Kypselos had blessed. Tyranny always broke one ruling class, but it would be a great mistake to suppose that it did not create another or that the other was any less tenacious than its predecessor.

The picture becomes clearer. A small number of men wanted power and seized it; a much larger number, in exchange for concessions which we cannot wholly grasp, was prepared to let them have it. But why did they want it? There is such a thing as power for its own sake; there is also such a thing as the belief that power should rest in a limited number of hands but that it should be distributed by rule (a standard of merit or wealth) rather than by accident of birth. But the most important facet of the first is that the power should be publicly recognised (and this is difficult under a tyranny); and it is essential to the second that there should be some form of constitution (which there was not under a tyranny). Thus we are almost forced to conclude that power was desired not *per se* or in principle but in order to do something; something that the Bakchiads refused to do.

What that was we do not know but a guess will illustrate the kind of policy disagreement that might have forced the issue. Here Pheidon of Argos reappears. He was killed, it is said, in a faction fight in Korinth, 'helping his friends', and there can be little doubt that the Bakchiads were not his friends. Under them Korinth had been the ally of Chalkis, Samos and Sparta during the Lelantine war and no one could be close both to Sparta and to her inveterate

enemy Argos. That the Spartan connection was maintained is strongly suggested by the story that some Bakchiads, on their expulsion, fled to Sparta; that they were Pheidon's enemies by the tale, already mentioned, of an Argive plot against Korinth, foiled by an informer. But since Pheidon's death and Kypselos' accession occurred in the same period it is likely that he died in precisely those disturbances which brought Kypselos to power, and, in that case, his 'friends', if not the Bakchiads, should be the friends of Kypselos. Once more we have to turn to Ephoros' unsupported story for detail. Kypselos, he says, spent his exile at Olympia, object of Pheidon's attention in 668 when he seized the sanctuary; more significantly, from Olympia Kypselos moved to Kleonai, a city of

A bronze lioness of Korinthian
workmanship found in Kerkyra; second
quarter of the sixth century.
The beast is basically of
Assyrian type (pages 80 and 81)
but Greek fantasy has left its mark on it.

the Argolid now under Pheidon's control, and from there returned
to Korinth. Altogether a very suitable route for a man on his way
to power as Pheidon's puppet – if only we could be sure he ever
took it. But where reliable detail fails, a general argument may help.
After Pheidon's great defeat of Sparta at the Battle of Hysiai in
669, the Delphic Oracle gave its support to Argos and consequently
must have broken its old ties with Sparta, and, one would imagine,
with Bakchiad Korinth. A few years later, as we have seen, the
Oracle gave its blessing to Kypselos. I do not believe that it would
have dared to do this without Pheidon's approval. Finally both
Pheidon and Kypselos were, I am sure, pro-hoplite, and, although
the hoplite revolution did not produce a hoplite creed, still less a
Hoplite-International, this must mean that to some extent they
shared a similar outlook. It is not implausible to suggest that this
similarity made them allies, and, if anyone feels that Kypselos was
too great a man to act as another's agent, that Korinth under him
was too successful to be in any way a dependency of Argos, he
need only remember that Pheidon died and that his successors
proved sadly inadequate to defend his empire.

If it were true that Kypselos was Pheidon's man we should expect a new look in Korinthian foreign policy under the tyrants, and

although for Kypselos history is blank, his son, Periander, certainly appears in, for a Korinthian, strange company. He had ties with Egypt, shared, among mainland Greek states, only with Aigina, which in Pheidon's day and perhaps still was a dependency of Argos. Much more significantly he was a close friend and ally of the tyrant Thrasyboulos of Miletos (he it was who advised the lopping of the ears of corn) and Miletos had been Korinth's enemy in Bakchiad days. It does not follow, of course, that Kypselos had set the example, still less that he came to power among other things as champion of a new foreign policy, but it is a reasonable conjecture.

Conclusion

Whether it's worth going through so much to learn so little is, as Mr Weller said of matrimony, a matter of opinion. But this discussion was not intended to search out the precise issues involved in the Korinthian political crisis so much as to emphasise yet again that those issues even among the active politicians may have been far more immediate, far more practical, far more accidental than we who generalise about Greek history are inclined to think they were. Little men probably followed Kypselos because a Bakchiad had pushed them off the pavement or jumped, when drunk, on a pile of their precious pots or fined them a sheep for an offence which had only brought their neighbour a caution; big men probably followed Kypselos because their followers were always fined a sheep while Bakchiad followers got away with a caution; because they wanted to squash Kerkyra when Bakchiads would not let them or make friends in Egypt or Miletos. The difference between the ordinary Korinthian of 657 and the ordinary Korinthian of 700 was not that he had acquired a new political doctrine which insisted on a wider distribution of power or an impartial system of justice but that he now resented the absence of justice as he did not before; that he no longer took it for granted that a drunken Bakchiad could break a pot; and, most important of all, that he could now see an

Terracotta statuette
of a man holding a cup;
ripe Korinthian period
(late seventh century).

alternative to Bakchiad government, an alternative almost as noble as the Bakchiads themselves and just as rich, men already obviously favoured by the gods who could easily persuade him that they had been granted the ultimate favour, that Zeus had decided at last to punish 'the judges who grind men down' and had appointed human agents for the job (agents who with Zeus and 5,000 hoplite spears behind them could easily deal with 300 Bakchiads who had neither a better god nor better arms). There was no direct evidence for Zeus' views but Apollo at least had spoken from Delphi on Kypselos' behalf as he had spoken twenty years or so before for Gyges of Lydia; and if anyone lacked absolute faith in Apollo's word there was solid comfort in the fact that Gyges had killed a king without the heavens falling, and Lydia was no worse off than it had ever been.

This discussion of tyranny in Korinth has not produced any clear definition of the issues at stake in seventh-century Greek politics. It would be misleading if it did. But it does help us to define the questions we should put to the evidence.

First of all we must always ask how far down through society the desire for political power had spread. At this date the answer is likely to be that it had not spread very far. Indeed, in class terms, it seems probable that it had not spread at all – the politically active in 650 were still the same kind of men as the *basileis* of 750; they may have been more numerous than the *basileis*; they may have stood for a different immediate policy for their state; they may have had different friends; they may have had different interests; but neither policy, friends nor interests were necessarily, in the case of Korinth even probably, of a fundamentally different kind.

Secondly, since the force behind the revolution was provided by a very much wider body, the hoplites, the problems of their discontent, of their claims must be kept quite distinct from that of political power.

Thirdly, since politics is always more concerned with the immediate, the practical, the specific than with abstract principle and in a society where theory scarcely exists is not only concerned with these things in fact but is clearly seen to be so, we must not expect a general pattern to appear at any superficial level, or indeed at any level of which contemporary Greeks themselves were aware nor should we be disappointed if the evidence speaks only of the particular villainy of this or that aristocrat, the private ambition of this or that revolutionary. On the contrary it would be surprising if the revolutions in Korinth, Sparta, Argos, Mytilene, Athens, Sikyon and all the rest had obvious characteristics in common, even more surprising if they were obvious at the time. But, although the historian has no more delicate job than to decide how far he should go beyond the obvious, no one would deny him the right to look a little further than the end of Kleopatra's nose. And if there should be anything in the evidence which points that far, he must make all he can out of it. Two words in a Delphic Oracle may seem a trifle on which to hang so much speculation, but, if my interpretation of them is correct, the astonishing thing is that there are even two. At the very least they justify our asking if specific grievances or specific quarrels are symptoms of some general feeling, whether consciously recognised as general or not. If pressed they may even suggest that they were.

5 Revolution in Sparta

The date

In one way the example of Korinth does help to provide positive information on the revolution. It gives one fixed point between the first signs of economic awakening in the early eighth century and the comparatively well-documented story of political development which begins with Athens in the late seventh. By 657 BC in a state which had been among the leaders of the economic revolution, the resulting upheaval had produced a sufficient amount of confusion among the aristocracy to bring a different section of that class to power; it had given them and a large enough number of lesser men sufficient independence to conceive of and welcome the possibility of change; and it had given the lesser men the weapons with which to effect the change.

Pheidon, the tyrants of Sikyon, Megara or Miletos, though roughly or even exactly datable, are much too shadowy to provide any such fixed point except on the assumption, which I should certainly make, that their background was much the same, but it is an assumption, and they throw no fresh light on the nature of the development; on the other hand Sparta, the one state which does tell us something about the desires of ordinary men, presents, at the same time, one of the most tricky chronological problems in Greek history.

At some early date Sparta acquired a constitution, the work, it was said, of a great law-giver, Lykourgos. But at first glance the ancient evidence shows little agreement about this early genius – so little that many modern historians, in even deeper despair than one Greek historian who finally decided to postulate two *Lykourgoi*, have simply dismissed the man himself as a fiction and relied on their intuition to fix the date of 'his' work. For us the identity of the law-giver is unimportant – someone devised a Spartan constitution and we may as well call him Lykourgos – but the date does matter and fortunately the problem, though perhaps insoluble, is not nearly so complicated as has been supposed. Most of the divergent dates in the authorities are the result either of the use of different chronological systems (chronology was another fifth-century invention) or of the propaganda battle that was later fought over Sparta's oligarchic stability (above, pages 12–3) and it is clear that in fact the bulk of the ancient evidence either dated or was consistent with the dating of Lykourgos to the reign of King Charillos, which must have covered, roughly, the years 775–750 and the dissentients, with one doubtful exception, place him even earlier.

The issue, then, is this. Can we accept law-making in Sparta in the early eighth century? Some modern scholars can, the majority find it impossible before the seventh, but even with them there is no agreement on the precise context. To some the second half of the seventh century seems preferable; to others, including myself, the years around 675. I cannot discuss the evidence here; it must suffice to set out the general considerations which make the traditional early date impossible and to consider, very briefly, how the different later dates should affect the interpretation of the changes as a whole.

Our chief evidence for the nature of the reform is a document preserved by Plutarch in his life of Lykourgos, a document which he calls a *Rhetra* or 'law' but which he rather confusedly describes as an oracle delivered to the Spartans by Delphi (the language certainly has some oracular elements in it). The text embodies some of the main provisions of the new constitution:

(i) When a sanctuary has been set up to Zeus Sullanios and Athena Sullania, when the people has been drawn up in tribes and in *obai* and a *Gerousia* [or Senate] established with thirty members including the kings; (ii) meetings of the assembly shall be held from time to time on Apollo's feast-day between Babyka and Knakion; (iii) here questions shall be introduced and the *Gerousia* shall stand aside; (iv) the assembly of the people shall have the final say.

There follows what Plutarch regards as a later amendment:

(v) But if the people should speak with a crooked voice, the Elders (sc. the *Gerousia*) and the Leaders (sc. the Kings) shall dismiss them. (*Lykourgos*, 6)

At one point, in clause iv, the text is corrupt; where it is certain the meaning is often obscure (the word I have translated 'stand aside' has been variously rendered 'dismiss', 'refuse to introduce proposals', 'reach a final decision'); even where the meaning of the words is clear, the significance of them often escapes us (what exactly is a 'crooked' voice?) but the general drift is firm enough and is confirmed by some verses of the mid-seventh-century Spartan poet, Tyrtaios, who seems to have summed up the new constitution in one poem, the bulk of which is unfortunately lost:

They listened to Apollo and brought home from Delphi the oracle of the God, his sure words. . . . 'The kings who are honoured by the gods shall show the way in counsel, they and the Elders, wise in years, whose care is lovely Sparta. After them the men of the people answering with straight decisions . . . ' (Fragment 4).

Now it is just possible to conceive of a defined constitution such as this existing in an unlettered world, waiting to be written down when Greeks recovered the art of writing about 750 BC but it is far more likely that the document should be contemporary with the institution of the system which it describes, and 750 therefore becomes a *terminus post quem* for the revolution. Tyrtaios, on the other hand, cannot have written much outside the years 680–620 BC. Hence the limits 750–620.

Again Tyrtaios ascribes the oracle to Delphi and although we cannot be certain that Tyrtaios is talking of the whole document or that he is telling the truth (in later centuries Delphi attracted much activity to which it had no real claim), the text itself is probably oracular in origin and Delphi, which had been Sparta's friend from its earliest days, is the obvious source. But we now know that Delphi did not exist as an oracular centre before the mid-eighth century. So the upper limit is confirmed.

Finally and decisively, the new constitution recognised a citizen body of some 9,000 'Equals' (this from other sources) who were to form the assembly. This can only be the Spartan hoplite army. But 9,000 Spartan hoplites did not exist before, at the outside, 725 and cannot have become a coherent political force before, again at

the outside, 700. So the limits are narrowed. Whatever the origin of the tradition associating Lykourgos with King Charillos, however firmly held by the Greeks themselves, it must be abandoned.

Had Sparta been, in every respect, a normal Greek state we should have had no difficulty in moving on to a more precise date, between 660 and 620. It would be almost unthinkable that a lesser city than Korinth should have outstripped her by much in political development. Indeed the nearer we could get to 620 and the later we could make Tyrtaios, the happier we should feel. But Sparta was abnormal in two important ways.

Like Korinth, she was a Dorian city but unlike Korinth (as far as we can tell) she had retained some of her primitive Dorian tribal customs (common messes for her citizens; an elaborate tribal

The plain of Sparta seen from the site of the ancient city. In the background Mount Taygetos which separates Lakonia from Messenia (see map on page 129).

– rather than family – education for her young), this perhaps explained by the fact that, unlike Korinth, she was surrounded by a number of surviving non-Dorian communities which she gradually incorporated or reduced to something approaching servile status, so providing herself with a valuable, but potentially dangerous, subject population, the so-called Helots, which she could exploit but which she had to guard herself against. From an early date Spartans were surrounded by a large body of men from whom they felt distinct and such a feeling of distinction easily leads to a feeling of community and consequently to a blurring of distinctions inside the privileged group. So it is readily understandable that Spartans could develop a greater sense of 'belonging' earlier than Korinthians and that they might therefore demand recognition of this belonging sooner than their other Dorian or non-Dorian fellows.

Secondly, like Korinth, she went through an economic revolution in the eighth century. But although, as far as we can tell, she had been open to all the same influences and pressures which provoked change elsewhere she had not reacted to them in the same way. Instead of solving her problems by colonisation, trade and manufacture she indulged in a war of conquest against the neighbouring territory of Messenia, the SW. Peloponnese, and by 715, having already conquered much of the SE., i.e. the later Lakonia, doubled her agricultural land by its annexation. From then on Sparta could prosper without the aid of commerce; she had committed herself to an almost exclusively agricultural future. The results were twofold. For one thing, although it is unlikely that a conflict of economic interest played any direct and significant part in the Korinthian crisis the mere existence of two interests, agricultural and commercial, however intertwined, must necessarily exacerbate any other tensions that there may be and it is undoubtedly true that the political trouble in Korinth was ultimately the result of the introduction of the new commercial element. It was not introduced into Sparta and could not therefore cause or exacerbate these tensions there. All Spartans were farmers and remained farmers. To that extent they had less to quarrel about than

Korinthians and we should expect their quarrels to be milder if they ever arose.

At the same time Korinthian prosperity came gradually, starting with a tentative probing towards the west after 800, growing steadily through the days of colonisation and more quickly thereafter with the increase of trade and manufacture which followed it. Sparta's wealth was won on the day she completed the conquest of Messenia's fertile plain and was spread among the whole Spartan population, unequally no doubt, as soon as that plain was divided up.

The suddenness of Spartan expansion and the peculiarity of Spartan society could, then, explain why the revolution there came early – as early as, say, 675; the homogeneity of this same society and of its economy could explain why the revolution was achieved without much bloodshed, without the destruction of the aristocracy, without the installation of a tyrant. The reader must judge for himself from the books mentioned in the bibliography whether the detailed evidence supports this *a priori* justification of a date early in the seventh century. The discussion which follows is based on the belief that it does; if it does not, some detail will have to be altered and Spartans will lose some, though by no means all, of the credit which I am about to give them – they will learn by others' mistakes rather than set an example which others failed to follow. But in either case the basic nature of the revolution is the same and in either case the revolution belongs to the same wider context – that of the seventh-century growth of hoplite self-confidence.

The changes

The Sparta which conquered Messenia was ruled by two kings from different families, the Agiadai and the Eurypontidai, a strange institution which the Spartans traced back to the twin sons of an early leader but is more probably to be explained by some earlier compromise between and coalition of rival Dorian groups. Beneath them an aristocratic council, the *gerousia*, then the free Spartan farmers and finally a largely non-Dorian labour-force, the helots.

Sparta was founded *c.* 950 BC. By 750 it controlled the Eurotas valley, by 715 eastern Messenia to which the rest was soon added. It was not until the middle of the sixth that she established a firm grip on the eastern coast of Lakonia up to the Gulf of Argos and on the island of Kythera, this at the expense of Argos. Many coastal cities retained nominal but unreal domestic independence; almost all good land in the interior became Spartan.

● Megalopolis

MESSENIA

River Eurotas

PARNON MOUNTAINS

ARGOLIC GULF

● Sparta

L A K O N I A

MESSENIAN GULF

TAYGETOS MOUNTAINS

LAKONIAN GULF

SPARTA

| 0 | 5 | 10 | 15 | 20 |
Miles

| 0 | 5 | 10 | 15 | 20 | 25 | 30 |
Kilometres

KYTHERA

In later history this series was further complicated by the existence of a number of *perioikoi* ('dwellers round-about'), the inhabitants of other cities in Lakonia which, although technically self-governing, were in fact completely subject to Sparta. But at this date it is unlikely that Sparta was either strong enough or well-organised enough to have absorbed these men into her own system; no doubt their cities already acknowledged Spartan superiority but their status was probably nearer that of the satellite than the subject; they would impinge only rarely on Spartan affairs and we may ignore them. As political animals we may also ignore the helots – so long as we take care to remember that their existence posed a constant threat to Spartan security, a constant encouragement to internal unity and a constant supply of Spartan wealth.

The body of the citizens, to use a word that is still anachronistic, was organised on the common aristocratic pattern, in tribes (the three Dorian tribes) composed of phratries, whose leaders, no doubt, manned the *gerousia*. Each phratry maintained by the contribution of its members one (some historians would say more than one) public mess (*sussition*) for its adult males, in effect the barracks for its own fighting unit; each phratry handled the education of its children through a series of age-groups up till the time when they graduated to membership of the mess. How far these primitive customs had fallen into disuse by, say, 700 we do not know; nor do we know whether there had grown up substantial distinctions within the body of Spartans, whether, that is, some phratries had become depressed at the expense of others or whether within each phratry some members had grown too poor to maintain their position, now tolerated as hangers-on, or perhaps not tolerated and expelled, or even whether there had been some recent influx to the community which had not been admitted to full membership. But we do know that one of the chief elements in the change was the reaffirmation if not a tightening up of the system as a whole and the declaration that all Spartans should now begin again as equal members of equal groups with sufficient resources (an allotment of land provided by the state with helots to work it) to maintain themselves in that position. If they failed, it was their fault – they were expelled, they ceased to be what it is now almost right to call full citizens – but at least they started with a fair chance. The fact was advertised – the Spartans were now known as *Homoioi* – 'Equals'. Measures like this surely imply considerable disorder and considerable inequality before.

But although the old system was maintained, even rejuvenated, it was no longer based on the same tribal background. A Spartan remained a member of his tribe but he now became as well the member of a new unit called an *oba*, a unit based not on (a mythical) common ancestry but on residence, for the *obai* were the wards of the city of Sparta and those parts of the surrounding countryside where Spartans lived. Somehow or other an integrated system of local *obai* and ancestral tribes was built up out of the basic units, the messes. How this was achieved is completely uncertain. The number of the *obai*, their relationship with the tribes, how the messes were fitted in to either, whether the messes themselves remained either in principle or in practice unchanged – all this is dark. And as a result we have no way of knowing how the new system affected either the composition of the Spartan governing class or of what became under the new régime the Spartan citizen body. But that it did affect both can hardly be doubted.

The new ruling class

Tyrtaios appears to say (some vital words are missing) that the Oracle which proclaimed the broad lines of the new constitution was brought from Delphi by the Kings Theopompos (*c.* 720– perhaps *c.* 670) and Polydoros (*c.* 700–*c.* 665). Both kings later had a reputation as reformers, Theopompos as a rather unwilling supporter of change, Polydoros as a radical popular hero (he was even said to have been assassinated by a disgruntled aristocrat). These are some of the details that have to be abandoned with a later dating, but, if true, they suggest very strongly that these kings, like Pheidon in Argos, were making use of popular discontent to confirm their royal authority over the aristocrats. A view made more plausible by the fact that, at some date, probably in the reign of these same kings, a new magistracy was created, the Ephorate which must in origin have been designed as an aristocratic check on royal authority and indeed always retained some of its original flavour. Moreover the Oracle itself gives great prominence to the constitution of the *gerousia* under the new system while later authorities (among them Aristotle) emphasise again and again 'Lykourgos' ' interest in its composition and its powers. From now on its numbers were fixed at thirty (including the two kings) and its members were elected, though choice was for life and was limited to candidates over sixty years of age from a defined group of aristocratic houses. It would be strange if the imposition of these rules alone did not produce some new aristocratic faces in the *gerousia* of 674 and even stranger if this result was not intended.

In other words, in Sparta, as in Korinth, the struggle for power was being conducted at the highest level in society; the picture is complicated by the existence of the kings and, perhaps, of a rather more coherent and vocal *demos*; it is obscured by an almost complete lack of reliable detailed evidence (did Lykourgos, as Plutarch says, choose the first *gerousia* himself? genuine tradition or historian's guess?), but its subject is clear – a ruling class which had so lost its internal stability in the face of unaccustomed problems and pressures that one section was prepared to look outside for help in holding or winning domination over another.

The new 'demos'

The ruling class is easy enough to define both before and after the reforms – roughly the royal houses and those other families which provided or could aspire to provide members of the *gerousia*. The *demos*, on the other hand, was in a very real sense created by the reforms, and it is almost impossible to describe the elements of which it was made up, or the distinctions which were removed to create the 'Equals', impossible not only because the evidence is lacking but because we do not even know the kind of language to use in describing them. Was the desired equality simply the status of being a hoplite? Did Lykourgos, that is, create new hoplites by a redistribution of land? Or was it equality among existing hoplites? If the second, was the inequality simply one of wealth, poor hoplites against rich hoplites, or of status? If of status, was it between phratry-member and outsider or was it between or even inside the phratries? The only certainty is that to be a full Spartan after 675 meant more than simply not to be a helot, that a line was drawn around some 9,000 men who from now on were to have similar rights and similar duties. It is likely enough that some non-helots were still left outside; certain that provision was made for demoting failures from the 9,000 without robbing them of their freedom and possibly for promoting promising outsiders. But the exceptions are irrelevant. What matters is that the question, what is a citizen, had now become meaningful. The answer, a man who shared these rights and duties, who belonged to the society not just because he had a sense of belonging but because he could produce a list of his privileges and his commitments.

The latter were simple if not light. As a boy the Spartan had to endure the various unpleasant exercises prescribed in the training programme, until, if he passed successfully, he was admitted to the *sussition*; from then on he had to provide from his allotment of land the appropriate contribution in kind to maintain his membership and, as a member, he devoted himself entirely to further exercise when not actually showing in the field the military excellence the exercise was designed to produce. His life was that of a soldier in barracks. But in return he had his land, a number of helots to work it and to serve him. And, more important for us if not for him, he was a member of a community which did more than guarantee his physical survival.

Of his legal rights nothing is known (nor indeed of the Spartan legal system as a whole); Sparta was not given to advertising the details of her administration abroad, and much of it was conducted by precedent rather than according to any written code. But

Spartans believed that Lykourgos had first established the precedents and, although he was certainly lauded as the originator of much in later Sparta which would have surprised him greatly, his reputation as the creator of her legal code cannot be entirely baseless. Details hardly matter; at least it is certain that he laid down some laws, that after 675 the Spartan knew what was expected of him and, more important, precisely what would happen to him if he failed to do it, knew too that the same was expected of everyone else and that the same penalties would be exacted. Even without evidence it is a safe assumption that he had not known this before.

Like the Korinthian the Spartan had his city 'set to rights' and it is a curious and comforting coincidence that the very words used by our sources, good and bad, to describe Bakchiad wickedness and Kypselos' virtue, reappear in the sources, good and bad again, for Sparta. The Bakchiads were men 'who used force', who 'exceeded the rule' and Kypselos won support against them by his generosity in administering the law; Polydoros, the reforming king, according to Pausanias, 'neither used violence nor exceeded the rule in word or deed but maintained strict justice tempered with kindness in conducting cases in the courts'. Pausanias, a guide-book writer of the second century AD, is never better than his source and in this case the quality of his source is unknown; but a poet who visited Sparta in 675, Terpander of Lesbos, has left two lines describing the Sparta of his day, I would say the new Sparta which Lykourgos had created:

> Spear-points of young men blossom there:
> Clear-voiced the Muse's songs arise:
> Justice is done in open air
> The help of gallant enterprise.
>
> (Tr. Sir Maurice Bowra)

'Justice' again has overtones which the Greek '*dike*' (the noun behind *dikaios*; p. 111) probably lacked in the seventh century; the emphasis again is on the existence of laws rather than on their quality and the same idea is reflected in another word used by contemporary Spartans (by Tyrtaios for example) to describe their new condition – *eunomia*, 'good order'. Law where there had been no law; order in place of disorder, and in this case we can be fairly sure that the ordinary Spartan actually wanted both.

The use of *eunomia* in the propaganda strongly suggests that they did – Tyrtaios was not writing only for the aristocrats; the ostentatious introduction of 'Equality' almost proves it, for this equality can hardly have been simply economic – all Spartans received an allotment of land, perhaps an equal allotment, but it is hard to believe that the rich lost everything they already held above the new minimum. It can only mean equality of status, not in all respects because just as there were rich and poor in later Sparta so there were aristocrats and commoners, but at least in some respects that mattered to ordinary men. Of these equality before the law is an obvious, almost necessary example.

It is still impossible to see how the seventh-century Spartan would formulate his demands for justice; quite impossible to know whether he also made demands for some political recognition, although this too he did receive. The text of the *Rhetra* enjoins the reorganisation of the citizen body by tribes and *obai*; also the new constitution of the *gerousia*; but it then goes on to appoint and regulate procedure for fixed meetings of a citizen assembly and, although the text at this point is corrupt, appears to affirm that this assembly should be sovereign; the final clause, probably as Plutarch says a later amendment, then seems to impose some restriction on this sovereignty.

Basically the form of constitution which is laid down here is typical of the developed constitutions of almost all later Greek states, oligarchic or democratic, where a comparatively small council conducted the day-to-day administration, prepared business for and presided over the deliberations of a sovereign assembly. There were vast differences between states in the membership and competence of both Council and Assembly but the pattern was constant and it first appears in Sparta. Not unnaturally some historians have been led to confuse form with content and have gone on to write as if Sparta too achieved together with the system some

A Spartan hoplite of mid-sixth century. The figure is rough and militaristic enough to give some superficial support to the traditional view of the dour, austere, barrack-like Sparta, supposedly created by Lykourgos. But it has some merit and, with the much jollier examples of Spartan art in the next three figures, suggests that Sparta had not yet settled down to a crabbed and gloomy devotion to empty militarism and conservative politics.

form of democracy in embryo and consequently to argue that if they achieved it they also wanted it. To some extent both steps are justified but I am not sure that it is to any significant extent.

To put the case against in an extreme form: neither democracy nor a constitutional oligarchy exists without democratic or constitutionally oligarchic spirit and it is at least as true that form encourages the growth of spirit as that spirit creates the form. In Sparta even within the circle of the 'Equals' there is very little sign that the assembly ever became conscious of its apparent theoretical power, that it ever acquired much spirit. If the final clause of the *Rhetra* is a later restriction on the power of the assembly, then the assembly was prepared to accept it. And when the assembly was consulted what form did the consultation take? 'Questions shall be introduced and [on my hesitantly offered translation] the *gerousia* shall stand aside; the assembly . . . shall have the final say.' What process does this imply? On two later occasions where we have a comparatively full account of procedure at an assembly, one in the fifth century (Diodoros, xi, 50), one in the third (Plutarch, *Agis*, ix–xi), neither of them wholly unambiguous or reliable, it would seem that the *gerousia* puts forward a question for discussion but not for decision and then holds a separate meeting ('stands aside'?) at which it formulates a proposal under the influence of the 'sense' of the assembly's reaction – under the influence of but not necessarily in accordance with the assembly's will. In fact in both cases, for special reasons, it seems to go against the assembly's will, and in both cases its decision seems to emerge in the end as established policy. All this is very much more like the activity of a Homeric assembly than of anything we know or imagine of later Greek democratic practice. Indeed throughout Spartan history there is no occasion on which the assembly is said to have taken any positive part in the direction of Spartan policy (as distinct from influencing that policy by its attitude).

It is just conceivable that an early sense of independence was gradually crushed by a consistently encroaching executive but it is far more likely that this independence never existed; that Spartans, unlike Athenians, simply failed to be trained by their constitutional forms into an awareness of what could be done with them, that in 675 they were delighted to meet and shout their approval or disapproval of this or that proposal put before them, as they did for centuries after, without ever realising that their shouts could or should be decisive, likely that they were, in fact, far nearer to the spirit of Homer's Ionian assembly than to anything we should find elsewhere in fifth-century Greece. If this is true another argument follows. There had no doubt been Homeric-type assemblies in Sparta before the time of Lykourgos; the only difference now was that they met by law, not at the whim of the kings or *gerousia*, hardly a major constitutional advance.

This, as I said, is an extreme form of the case. To prescribe assemblies *is* to do more than to convene them casually, much more; to affirm the sovereignty of the *demos* as the *Rhetra* does means something even if that sovereignty is never respected in any real sense and it is likely that both prescription and affirmation were welcomed even demanded by the average Spartan. But, as I see it, the answer lies in moving as little as possible from this extreme rather than as near as we can to the idea of full democratic responsibility, or vocal democratic agitation.

Conclusion

In the case of Korinth I offered a guess to illustrate the kind of political crisis which might have brought Kypselos to power. Perhaps I may be allowed to do the same for Sparta. Lykourgos and the kings I would imagine were concerned to alter the composition of the aristocracy. To do this they enlisted the support of the Spartan hoplite army with promises of land, justice and that way of life which the Spartans called *eunomia*. They kept their promises. They achieved their ends without destroying the existing aristocrats and the result at the start would have been a new governing class divided against itself; it would be too much to ask that the old should give way without a struggle to the new. In such a situation

A mid-sixth century Spartan cup. Arkesilas, king of Kyrene in N Africa with which Sparta had fairly close contacts, superintends the weighing of some merchandise. The overall effect is rather fussy but the scene is full of life and is especially interesting both as being contemporary and not narrowly Spartan.

the continued support of the hoplites might seem vital and this could be assured by providing a regular means of demonstrating the support to any opposition – the assembly (it is always easy to encourage popular feeling when it is in your favour). But once the initial question of status inside the aristocracy was settled common agricultural interests, a common fear of helots, possibly even the beginnings of a common suspicion of the hoplites might well bring a quick merging of the old and new; quite soon the *gerousia* could have seen that it was politic to present a solid front, to settle

A Spartan cup of the third quarter of the
sixth century, the last period of respectable
Lakonian pottery. Spartan artists were
especially keen on human figures in general
and on revellers (komasts) in particular. This
is an exceptionally restrained example.

its disagreements without appeal to popular opinion. Meanwhile a
happy accident may have helped to crush any hoplite independence
that there was. In 669 BC Polydoros led out the new army in an
attack on Argos and the new army was decisively beaten by the
Argives under Pheidon at the Battle of Hysiai. Just as the Athenian
disaster in Sicily in 413 brought temporary disgrace on the democracy that had voted for the expedition, so it is easy to see how
defeat might break the confidence of the Spartan hoplite, particularly as that defeat was immediately followed by a long and desperate struggle against a Messenian revolt, a struggle which could
not but unite all Spartans.

So, perhaps, the Spartan aristocracy survived the crisis which
broke so many of the other aristocracies of Greece; the economic
and social demands of the hoplites had been satisfied, the political

A bronze statuette of a running girl. Probably of Spartan workmanship, found in Albania. About 500 BC. As is also shown by the great bronze bowl recently found at Vix, Spartan bronzeworkers retained their inspiration at least until the end of the sixth century, i.e. after their potters had given way before Attic competition (see page 181).

demands were not and because of Sparta's peculiar position never became so pressing that another revolution could be built around them alone; the concessions made in 675 did not materially alter the distribution of power inside the state – they could be absorbed, perhaps in part ignored, perhaps even withdrawn (by the final clause of the *Rhetra*) without trouble. When King Polydoros was assassinated by an aristocrat, his murderer was honoured with a tomb in Sparta and Pausanias, who reports it, was surprised – 'either the assassin had been a good man before or possibly his relatives buried him secretly' (iii, 3). Rather, I should think, the Spartans had forgotten what they owed and did not realise what might have been owed to their king.

6 Revolution in Athens: Solon

The impact of Sparta

The importance of the Spartan revolution then was not so much in what it did for Sparta and its *demos* as in the example that it set for the rest of Greece; and the important part of the example was not so much that the general pattern of the constitution defined in Sparta was adopted elsewhere as the simple fact that a constitution had been defined. It may be that some other state gave her the idea – there is a strong tradition that Lykourgos modelled his laws on those of Krete and one Kretan city at least had an assembly functioning before the end of the seventh century. But we know nothing of the date or nature of its institution. It may be that the priests at Delphi had some hand in formulating the scheme which Lykourgos finally imposed – again the tradition is strong and the *Rhetra* certainly had Delphic blessing if not inspiration. A little later (when Sparta was already turning her back on Polydoros and Lykourgos?) Delphi supported the hoplite champions Pheidon and Kypselos. Or both Delphi and Krete might have played a part – they were close to each other at this date and Apollo's priests were said to be of Kretan origin. Perhaps the idea even came from further afield – assemblies of a sort may already have been known in the Phoenician cities and, much later, the Phoenician colony at Karthage appears with a constitution not unlike the Spartan (or the Kretan). But, whatever the ultimate origins, Sparta remains the first state in Greece which we know consciously to have created a new social and political system with an authority greater than that of any member or class of members of the state. For us she is the inventor of the idea of constitutional government and virtually of the idea of a citizen. Both ideas were catching.

The rest of the century is thick with law-givers, Zaleukos of Italian Lokroi, Charondas at Katana in Sicily, Androdamas of Rhegion and others but none is much more than a name to us. We can see, though, that they are concerned with the same two problems, with the definition of a citizen (shown in their interest in land-tenure) and in the formulation of a law-code. Even one tyrant

A section of one of the most famous (because most complete) law-codes in antiquity, the Gortyn code. The code was inscribed in twelve columns on the curved inner wall of a building, probably a lawcourt, at Gortyn in Krete around 450 BC. The text is *boustrophedon*, i.e. alternate lines are read from left to right and right to left, a primitive style which survived so late only in backward areas. The code itself, however, is by no means primitive.

was affected. In Lesbos one of the aristocratic factions finally turned to the people for support and chased its rivals abroad. But the result was not tyranny; it was a publication of the laws and, of all things, a ten-year tyranny from which the tyrant quietly stepped down. If we knew more of these law-codes we should doubtless be horrified by their crudity and their brutality, but that is not the point. What matters is that something, no matter what, is on the record, is defined. There is an appeal to something beyond the individual magistrate; there is also a chance to study what it is and to conceive of the possibility of change.

Kylon and Drakon

The whole process can be followed in some detail at Athens. Athens had survived the Dorian invasion unconquered and, although her Mycenaean civilisation collapsed in the following economic crisis almost as completely as that of other less fortunate Mycenaean centres, she may have retained throughout some kind of hold over the surrounding area, over the peninsula we call Attika, which helped her to make a quicker recovery than was possible elsewhere. At least she took the lead in the development of what is known as protogeometric pottery (roughly between 1000 and 900 BC) and by 750 BC her geometric ware was finer than anything else the Greek world could produce. But this same comparative sophistication and, even more, her comparative richness in cultivable land, robbed her of the incentive for territorial expansion which affected Korinth or in a different way, Sparta. Athens sent out no colonies nor did she annex her neighbours' land. As a result she suffered a comparative decline during the seventh century; the eclipse of her pottery by that of Korinth in the seventh century is just a symptom of a general collapse.

In 630 BC Attika was still ruled by a narrow group of aristocratic families; they called themselves the *Eupatridai*, the 'well-born', and they traced their superiority back to a day when a Mycenaean king of Athens, Theseus, had called together the best of Attika's local chiefs to form his council. This council, called the Areopagos, had long since disposed of the kings as it had exaggerated, no doubt, its own stability and antiquity. But now its authority was complete.

But even the purest agricultural economy cannot avoid some taint of commerce in a commercial world and as we can see, for example, in Africa today even the most backward society will be influenced by ideas that are current around it. About 630 there was an attempt to set up a tyranny in Athens – a young nobleman,

Kylon, supported by his father-in-law, the tyrant of neighbouring Megara, and by the oracle at Delphi seized the Akropolis with the support of Megarian troops. No doubt this foreign backing robbed him of some local sympathy – but Kypselos, if I am right, had not found this a serious hindrance. Rather the failure of Kylon's *coup* must be due to a lack of widespread and/or serious discontent – an assembly was called by the magistrates and it gladly left the suppression of its would-be champion to those magistrates (this is just the kind of occasion on which an assembly might be useful). Kylon and his supporters were executed although they had been promised their lives.

But there was some discontent; some quite serious tension in Athenian society. By chance the chief magistrate of the year, Megakles, belonged to a family which played a leading part in every Athenian political crisis for the next two hundred years, the Alkmeonids. Aristocrats of the bluest blood (*Eupatridai*, of course) they are often described as rogue aristocrats, a family outside the general run of the nobility with dangerous radical tendencies. But this is an exaggeration. Some great radical 'rogues' of the fifth century, Perikles among them, were connected with the family but none was a member of it; Kleisthenes, the radical reformer of 508 was a member but, I am sure, was only radical because he had to be (see pp. 191–203); in 594 they did indeed support the progressive programme of Solon but even this may have been of necessity rather than conviction, necessity born of this earlier crisis. For Megakles was attacked for his treacherous murder of Kylon and the bulk of the aristocracy gladly joined in condemning what they had no doubt approved at the time, in recognising the curse which Delphi placed on the family and in expelling it from Attika.

About the same time, some ten years after Kylon's death, Drakon drew up and published the first Athenian law-code. What intrigues brought disgrace to the Alkmeonids, what pressures brought Drakon into action, we do not know – but it would be odd if they were totally unlike those that we have already studied elsewhere or totally unconnected with the Kylonian crisis.

Drakon's laws have acquired some reputation for severity and no doubt they were severe by later standards, just as they were probably incomplete and crude ('They contained nothing remarkable but the harshness of the penalties' says Aristotle, looking down his sophisticated nose.) (*Politics* 1274 b 16), but they cannot have been more crude or more severe than the average arbitrary decision of a Eupatrid judge. More important, whatever their character, they offered, like the efforts of those other earlier law-givers, a formulation of the law which merely by its existence made criticism and alteration possible. The more severe it was, the sooner and more violent the criticism would be. Fortunately in Drakon's case we at last get some hint of how this criticism and alteration came about.

Debt and the 'hektemoroi'

In Attika around 600 BC there existed a large number of small farmers who were, in some way or other, bound to a wealthier master. These men were called *hektemoroi*, 'sixth-parters' and this almost certainly means that they had to pay their overlord one-sixth of their annual crop (the alternative suggestion that they paid five-sixths goes against the best evidence (Aristotle) and is an impossibly high figure). If they failed they and their families could be sold into slavery. In this case the land they worked, the status of which had been indicated by the placing on it of a *horos* or 'marker', passed, presumably, into the hands of the master.

At the same time it is clear that there was an acute problem of debt and by existing law all debts were secured on the personal freedom of the borrower. Thus, like the *hektemoros*, the debtor who failed in his obligation to repay could become a slave.

Both problems were solved in 594 BC when Solon was elected archon (chief magistrate), mediator and law-giver, and passed his *seisachtheia*, 'the shaking-off of burdens', by which the status of *hektemoros* was abolished, existing debts cancelled and the use of the person as security forbidden for the future.

In trying to explain the crisis and its solution the ancient sources, Aristotle again, and Plutarch in his *Life of Solon*, appear to connect the *hektemoros* with debt and this connection has been accepted and indeed developed by most modern historians who start the small free farmer on the path to slavery via hektemorage by borrowing from his richer neighbour (neither Plutarch nor Aristotle explicitly describes the origin of the status). But the result is an apparent contradiction. If all debts were contracted from the start on the security of the person, there is, logically, no room for the *hektemoros*. Slavery should follow immediately on failure to repay the original loan. Besides, it is by no means easy to imagine the precise course of degeneration from debtor to *hektemoros* – at what point of indebtedness did the change take place? Did seventh-century Athenians never incur debts with more than one rich man? If they did, whose *hektemoros* did they become?

Many stories can be, many have been constructed to get round the difficulties but by far the most popular answer to the central, logical or legal, problem, has been the claim that land in Attika before Solon was the inalienable property of the family not of the individual. If it had been, the creditor might well find it more profitable to accept a man as a *hektemoros* and thus retain a constant profit from and some control of his land, rather than to sell him off as a slave and see the land revert to other members of his family. But there is no evidence whatsoever that land in Attika ever had been inalienable. The original allotments made by Lykourgos to the Spartans were, but Lykourgos had good reason to legislate for stability – the desire to maintain his 9,000 property-owning citizens. There are other examples too where the first allotment in a colony was similarly controlled but we know of no case of inalienability where there had not been at some stage an artificial distribution of holdings and we know of no artificial distribution in Attika – nor in Boiotia and there, as early as the eighth century, Hesiod could discuss the possibility of buying or selling a farm. No doubt, as in any primitive community, land in Attika was regarded as a family as well as an individual holding, no doubt the poor Athenian was in effect tied to his land by centuries of tradition, by sentiment, and by the brutal fact that he had nowhere else to go, but it takes more than tradition or sentiment to prevent expropriation by the all-powerful rich; if it is to their advantage it takes a law and of law there is no sign.

Fortunately, in rejecting this approach, there is now no need to look for any more plausible alternative along the same lines. For it has recently been pointed out that the whole problem may be an artificial one. Solon's abolition of debt would hold the imagination of later Greeks for whom debt was still a familiar worry while hektemorage, once abolished, would soon be forgotten, so that the fourth-century historian (and all our evidence comes directly or indirectly from the fourth century or later) might well find it difficult to disentangle genuine detail about it from a received tradition of general pre-Solonian indebtedness. And indeed there was general indebtedness in a sense (debt is not a very precise word): the *hektemoros* 'owed' one-sixth of his produce per annum as the borrower 'owed' the principal and interest on his loan and both suffered the same legal penalty, slavery, if they defaulted. But it need not follow from this identity of penalty or superficial similarity of relationship that the 'contract', as it were, by which a man accepted hektemorage, was entered into because he was *already* in debt.

There is a parallel for such a 'contract' in Genesis chapter 47 where, the story goes, the Egyptians, having bought food from Joseph in the first years of the famine with their money and their cattle –

came unto him . . . and said . . . There is not ought left in the sight of my lord, but our bodies and our lands . . . And Joseph bought all the land of Egypt for Pharaoh . . . and said unto the people, Behold, I have bought you this day and your land for Pharaoh: lo, here is seed for you, and ye shall sow the land. And it shall come to pass in the increase, that ye shall give the fifth part unto Pharaoh, and four parts shall be your own.

Whatever the truth in this tale, the Israelites who later formulated it could at least conceive of such a transaction, a transaction which produced a kind of hektemorage without any pre-existing debt. The motive there was indeed economic pressure and in Attika it could have been the same, but not necessarily so. Simple fear, a need for physical protection in the uncertain conditions of the Dark Ages might have made small men glad to submit to a powerful neighbour, offering in exchange not only loyalty and service (above, p. 49) but a regular payment in kind. In time the need for protection would disappear but not the desire to 'protect' nor the power to insist on protecting and on the payment for it. A more or less casual arrangement for mutual advantage could become a fixed and inherited relationship and at some stage or other this relationship was sanctioned by law; the standard contribution implied by the word *hektemoros* can hardly have grown up by accident.

Whether or not it was Drakon who first defined it, who therefore invented the word *hektemoros*, is relatively unimportant; if he was responsible for any general presentation of Athenian law he cannot have failed to take this kind of bondage into account, he must have been the first to set out in writing the rules which governed it, just as he must have been the first to do the same for the laws of debt. In that case it is hard to believe that the pre-Solonian agitation was not in large part due to the fact that Drakon had for the first time brought both *hektemoroi* and debtors face to face with the full implications of their position.

Causes of discontent: the poor

That this might have been the case has long been recognised but the traditional view of the *hektemoros* as a defaulted debtor and the failure to admit explicitly enough that the status, whatever its origin, could have been and probably was a long-standing one, inherited perhaps through generations or even centuries, have persuaded historians that they must look for some fairly immediate reason for the late-seventh-century agitation and that this reason should be in itself or in its effects economic; more simply, that there

This view of the Akropolis from the west gives some impression of the Attic plain and of Athens' relation to it. A mile or two to the east rises Hymettos; three or four miles to the NE (centre left) is Pentelikon; due north (off the photograph) is Parnes. Three small rocky hills, the Akropolis itself, Lykabettos (hidden behind the Akropolis) and Tourkovouno (left foreground) are the only interruptions in this flat and not infertile stretch.

must have been some special crisis of poverty, debt and consequent enslavement in the neighbourhood of 600 BC.

Many suggestions have been made: a gradual impoverishment of the Attic soil through overcropping, reaching danger-point at this moment; a more accidental series of bad harvests or destructive foreign invasion (Athens was at war with Megara about this time); the introduction of coined money which would make it easier to borrow and more attractive to lend (coinage first appeared in Greece about 600 though there was no native Athenian coinage before about 570); and so on. Any or all of these could have been relevant and, of course, on any theory there must have been considerable economic distress around – debtors are men in trouble

The plain of Marathon, looking
inland from the Soros (figure on page 205).
The vast majority of the trees
are olives. Marathon belonged to
the *Hyperakria* (page 178) but is much
flatter and richer than most of it.

and there must have been a number of them; the *hektemoros* cannot have been a rich man to start with and the drain of annual payments could not leave many with any great chance of dramatic improvement. But, if I am right about the origin and nature of hektemorage, economic distress need be no more than part of the motive for revolution and, although it may have become suddenly more acute just before 600, it is not necessary that it should. The Russian peasant did not join the revolution of 1917 because of any immediate increase of hardship.

Indeed it is even possible that the class of *hektemoroi* as a whole was better off in 600 than it had ever been before, for Athens too had at last reached the stage of economic development that had transformed Korinth a century or more before. Her failure to join the colonial gold rush of the late eighth century can only be explained by her comparative prosperity at the time, by the amount of land which the early unification of Attika had given her, enough, it would seem, to absorb her own expanding population. The richer areas, the central plain around and to the north of Athens, the smaller plain of Eleusis, the Mesogaia (south-east of Hymettos), all these grew grain, enough to allow some export even as late as 600; elsewhere she had less fertile soil which was admirable for the olive and the vine. Those who grew them cannot have prospered much on domestic trade but during the seventh century a rich foreign market for her oil was discovered in the Black Sea area and although this was not the only factor in the great upsurge of Athenian economy before and after Solon it is undoubtedly an important one.

For more than two centuries after 600 Athens was prepared to fight for control of the Black Sea route as she was prepared to fight for nothing else. She was not fighting to preserve the market but to safeguard the supply of grain which the cornfields of south Russia produced in abundance and on which she soon came to depend but there can be little doubt that she always paid directly or indirectly for her grain with oil (later also with silver) not grown in Russia, or that the first moves she made to secure the route were at least in part provoked by a desire to sell as much as a need to buy;

an aristocratic government, composed of men whose own rich acres produced grain, does not cut its throat by fighting to admit competitors.

It is impossible to decide with certainty how soon or how extensively Athenians became involved with Russia in the seventh century. Other Greeks, from Ionia, may have settled on the south coast of the Black Sea in the mid-eighth century but it was not until the first half of the seventh that these same Ionians became seriously and regularly involved, not until near the end of it that the leading colonies on the north and west coast were established, at Apollonia Pontica, Istros at the mouth of the Danube, Berezan, Olbia, and elsewhere. But by the same time Athenians were engaged in a war against the city of Mytilene in Lesbos, another oil-producing state, for possession of a foothold in the Troad, at Sigeion, an obvious move towards the Black Sea, and at about the same time Athenian vases began to appear around these same approaches.

The distribution of a city's pottery is no sure guide to its trade in general; vases which we can identify were largely luxury goods which need not go in the same direction or at the same period as primary exports; some great trading cities indeed produced no vases at all. These finds are, then, no evidence for or against a developing trade in oil. But they are evidence that some Athenian products were moving towards the Black Sea (and they are not likely to have travelled alone) and they are also among the first signs that Athenians had discovered yet another commodity that could sell abroad. Since the middle of the century Athenian potters had begun to look at and learn from Korinthian models and by about 600 this foreign inspiration coupled with a fine local clay and even finer local genius was producing a ware that could match the best Korinthian achievements. During the next century Attic vases became the standard luxury pottery throughout the Mediterranean.

The men who benefited from an increased sale of pottery were unimportant potters; some might benefit enough to become important potters but none would become important men and there would never be more than a handful of them. But those who would gain from the beginnings of a trade in oil were farmers and although the bulk of the profits would go to a few with a substantial surplus from large estates, even the poorest smallholder is likely to have had an olive-tree or two in some rough corner of his plot and, thanks to the possibility of interplanting, all but the poorest might be able to make a gradual change (only gradual because olives are slow producers). Many might not make the attempt; many might make it and fail, finding themselves in debt as a result; but many more could find themselves marginally, some even substantially better off, particularly as there must always have been a tendency to grow more olives on less fertile, i.e. the poor man's soil.

The picture, then, of general agricultural depression is probably false and is certainly oversimplified, the insistence on poverty and debt as the only motives for discontent is probably misleading and it therefore becomes permissible to suspect that many of Attika's small farmers were irked by something other than fear of starvation or impending slavery, by the inferiority of their status as *hektemoroi*, an inferiority which became all the more galling when formally recognised and written into law by Drakon, that they were impelled to revolt not only by the fear of actual slavery but by the mere fact that, though Athenians, they *could* be enslaved. Athenians, perhaps, like Korinthians, had come to hate their masters in part because they were masters, not because they were rent-collectors, and, perhaps, like Spartans, wanted to be 'Equals'. Too little emphasis has been given to Aristotle's judgment on the crisis:

For the mass of the people the bitterest and the harshest element in their life as citizens was their *subjection* to the rich. This is not to say that they had no other grounds for complaint. (*Athenian Constitution*, 2)

Causes of discontent: the rich

But rich men too had grounds of complaint against some of their fellows. Some smallholders, as we have said, may have begun to make a profit by selling their surplus oil; how much more profit could be won by large landowners and especially by those whose

Men gathering the olive-crop,
on an Attic black-figure amphora
of the later sixth century
by the Antimenes painter.

estates were not ideal for grain-growing, that is by those aristocrats whose land lay in the less fertile parts of Attika, the north-east and the south-west coast. Within a decade or two men who had previously been rich only by local standards could find themselves the equals or even the superiors of the old aristocracy of the central plain. It was just such men who led the attack on the Eupatrid monopoly of power.

Some of them were themselves *Eupatridai*; as elsewhere the ruling class could not maintain its unity in the face of new pressures and in Attika with an aristocracy drawn originally from all parts of Attika, it is clear that divergent local interests played a big part in encouraging the break. The expulsion of the Alkmeonids after the Kylonian affair, Eupatrids though they were, is a sign of internal squabbling among the nobility and the Alkmeonids took their revenge and secured their return by supporting Solon. But there was more than a personal quarrel involved – it is almost certain that the family's original estates lay in hilly country near the south-west coast. Solon himself was also a Eupatrid; his family history is unknown but, we are told, they had grown poor and Solon had recouped his fortunes by trade – he had set himself apart from the traditional aristocracy. Close to Solon was the Eupatrid family of Peisistratos, the later tyrant; they too came from poorish land, this time near the east coast. Other names are attached to Solon's 'party' by more doubtful evidence; of them it is enough to say that as far as we know none comes from the central plains, some are definitely located elsewhere.

If further proof is needed it lies in the political squabbles which followed Solon's legislation. Three factions were then contending for political power. Peisistratos had broken with Solon and now led a party of his own – 'The men beyond the Hills' i.e. from north and eastern Attika (below, pp. 178–81). The rest of Solon's supporters were grouped behind the Alkmeonids as the '*Paralioi*' – the men of the south-west coast, Alkmeonid country. The third was the hard core of the Eupatrid caste – significantly 'The men of the Plain'.

I have insisted throughout that day-to-day politics do not directly reflect any underlying pattern of economic or social development and I do not want to suggest now that all those who joined in the struggle against the Eupatridai were olive-growing nobles and their olive-growing followers from further Attika or that every man loyal to the Eupatrid cause lived in the cornfields of the plain. Far from it. The Athenian crisis was a complex one. All ordinary men must have picked up something of the infectious independence that had been spreading over Greece for something like a century or more and in hektemorage they would see, whether *hektemoroi* themselves or not, an all too obvious challenge to that independence. Many of them, in all parts of Attika, were better off than they had ever been, hoplites, like the Spartans or Korinthians, and self-conscious enough to think that they deserved similar recognition in society. Many others again throughout Attika were desperately poor, debtors, near-debtors, some *hektemoroi* and others, and they too had their ambitions, freedom from the immediate threat of slavery or starvation, perhaps also a share of a rich neighbour's fields.

But political initiative still lay with the aristocrat and the aristocrat was still a local chief as well as a member of the national government, or rather, was a local chief whether or not he was lucky enough to be a member of the national government as well. To some extent his own interests would be the same as those of his followers but, even where they were not, aristocratic power can never be maintained if the aristocrat ignores altogether the welfare of his supporters. It is here, I would imagine, that the rise of this or that area of Attika would make itself felt; some aristocrats, a few who were Eupatrids, many who were not, would find their own estates more profitable than they had been before and would expect appropriate political recognition; others would find that their followers had acquired new interests, new claims, and, if suitably encouraged, the power to make an attempt to satisfy them. But even at this level there are complications. Obviously the men most likely to make use of supra-local discontents are those who, for local reasons, want change. But the shrewd entrenched Eupatrid might well himself exploit some general feeling to thwart the local revolutionary; and some outsiders could well feel that the possible political gain from a campaign, let us say to liberate the *hektemoroi*, would be inadequate compensation for the loss of his own *hektemoroi*.

In fact the evidence does not suggest that there were many substantial exceptions of this kind. The Eupatrids as a body were not clever enough to play off one discontent against another; when the trouble came they had to surrender on all fronts. But it would seem that they were wise enough to surrender in time and lucky enough to find the opposition led by a man who disapproved of violence and was still able to restrain the extremists among his followers. This was Solon.

Solon and the governing class

Solon is often described as a mediator, between noble and commoner, rich and poor. Such indeed was his official title when he was chosen as chief archon for 594 and given an extraordinary commission to revise the laws and the constitution. But the title should not mislead us into thinking that he stood between the two contending parties as an independent, as some sort of archaic Ombudsman, that his solution was a compromise. With a cynicism born of political innocence many refuse to believe that a party politician can be either wise or good; if Solon was both wise and good, as he clearly was, it follows that he was no party politician. But for every story in the sources which illustrates the virtuous sage there is another that shows the shrewd, partisan, and not always wholly honest operator and I am quite happy to believe that he was both at once; that he was no more neutral, no less of a committed politician than was, say, Ghandi. Nor is there any doubt what his party was. From his poems, in which he analysed the situation before his archonship and justified his measures after it, fragmentary and difficult though they are, it is clear that he identified himself entirely with the revolutionaries. He attacks the injustice, greed and pride of the princes; he threatens them 'Neither shall we obey you nor will all stay in order for you'; and Aristotle, for whom the poems were complete, could say 'in everything Solon consistently laid the blame upon the rich' (*Athenian Constitution*, 5). He himself could boast that he might have become a tyrant – men do not think of making an uncommitted moderate a tyrant. It is only afterwards that Solon boasted that he had been above party and even then it emerges that it is only one group among his followers whose demands he had ignored and that those demands were not so much for more extreme reform as for violence and confiscation. Of course to leave the Eupatrids alive and in possession of their estates did mean that the political changes were less drastic than they would otherwise have been but they were less drastic more because Solon disapproved of bloodshed than because he disapproved of change.

There is, then, no reason to think that Solon was not by contemporary standards an extremist or that he gave the average Athenian very much less than he wanted, except perhaps for a taste of blood and an extra acre or two. What he gave them, group by group, is, therefore, a fair guide to each group's ambitions. By his reforms the population was divided into the four classes, *pentakosiomedimnoi*, *hippeis*, *zeugitai* and *thetes* (defined above, p. 22). In a sense the last three had existed before – for a long time there had been Athenian cavalry, Athenian hoplites and Athenians who were neither; roughly the rich, the comfortable to ordinary and the ordinary to poor. The fourth, the *pentakosiomedimnoi*, was new but, in itself, of no great significance. Solon's fundamental innovation was in the use he made of the classification. From 594 onwards eligibility for public office was to depend not on membership of a family but on membership of a census class.

Some important financial posts were reserved for *pentakosiomedimnoi*, an obvious precaution – fear of losing 500 measures a year by confiscation would deter all but the most light-fingered treasurer. Otherwise the top two classes were probably treated as

Left. Figure of a woman holding a cup from Naukratis in Egypt; early sixth century. Commercial contact with Egypt began at about the same time as with the Black Sea, and Naukratis, the only settlement, dates from about 630 BC. The influence of Egyptian art, well illustrated here, was enormous.

Opposite. Figure of a young man holding a lotus sceptre
from Kameiros in Rhodes (*c.* 600 BC) showing marked Egyptian influence.
Rhodes was well placed to act as an intermediary in passing on
Egyptian ideas to Greece as a whole. But there was
much direct contact elsewhere; Solon himself visited Egypt and
is said to have taken over one Egyptian law.

one and high political office, the archonship, was open only to
them. So the Eupatrid monopoly of political power was broken,
and broken in such a way that Solon must have hoped no new
monopoly would be created; a marked contrast to tyrant Korinth.
Anyone in the future who reached the necessary status became a
potential politician. The immediate effect of the change would
depend on two things, on the number of men in the top classes
who were not Eupatridai and on the success the new men had in
exploiting the chance Solon had given them; unfortunately there is
no firm evidence on either.

It is hardly to be expected that Eupatridai would welcome the
outsiders without a struggle, even if they had been forced to accept
new rules which technically allowed them in, and for this struggle
they would have three powerful weapons. Firstly the old aristocratic Council, the Areopagos, recruited as it was from those who
had already held office, would still be, in 594, entirely Eupatrid.
Some of its members, no doubt, had supported Solon but the
majority had not, and it would take many years, even if non-
Eupatrids were elected to every archonship, before the composition
of the Council would properly reflect that of Solon's new governing
class. What powers the Areopagos had are far from certain, whether any of them could be used to influence elections totally unclear; but even if the constitutional rights of such a body are
minimal, its prestige is enormous (we need only compare the Roman Senate), and it is safe to assume that the greater part of that
prestige would be at the service of anyone who set out to undo or
stultify Solon's work.

Secondly there was the phratry system which Solon left un-
touched; so long as it provided the basic social and military organisation of the State, it must have retained as well some substantial
measure of that automatic obedience of the phratry-member for
the phratry-boss which made politics a game of pyramid-
manipulation not of class-appeal. The ordinary man could not
become an entirely free agent and the man who controlled the
phratry to some extent controlled its votes. It is true, of course,

One face of a *stele* from Chios carrying regulations for legal procedure. (*c.* 570 BC). There is mention of a Council, non-aristocratic like Solon's, and of the possibility of appeal (page 173). The lettering is again *boustrophedon* (cf. page 144). A paraphrase of this face: '. . . there shall be appeal to the popular Council which shall meet on the tenth of the month, chosen fifty from each tribe, and shall deal with the *demos*' business and the appeal cases . . .'.

that some of Solon's new men would be phratry-bosses on their own account and none can have lacked entirely some influence inside the system. But the system itself had grown up with, was wholly geared to Eupatrid domination, and in consequence it must surely still have operated in Eupatrid interests.

This being so the local distribution of Solon's support would also tell in Eupatrid favour. By 594 many nobles had probably acquired land and houses near the city and a local following; in any case their estates lay not very far away in the central plain. There might be many voters in and near the city who were prepared to act against Eupatrid orders, but there would also be many more loyal Solonians at Marathon or Sounion who could not face the walk to Athens to support their local leaders.

On the other hand the Solonian too had his weapons. In his study of the Athenian constitution (chapter 8) Aristotle claims that Solon introduced a curious and complicated electoral procedure for the archonship, a selection by lot of the nine men needed from a panel of forty candidates, elected ten from each of the four tribes. Unfortunately the same Aristotle in his *Politics* (1274 a 1) seems to contradict this, and, although the *Politics* is probably an earlier work and scholars can change their minds, they do not always change them for the better. There is no other substantial evidence, and argument, about the nature of Aristotle's evidence, about the credibility of the use of lot in this early context, and other things, does not lead to any firm conclusion. On balance I am inclined to believe that Solon did introduce sortition but without much confidence. If he did, however, there can be no doubt that it would help his purpose. It would be much less easy for Eupatridai to monopolise forty than nine places and, once on the short list, only luck stood between the new man and office.

But this is hypothetical. There is a much stronger case for Solon having instituted a new Council (of 400 members, 100 from each tribe), a forerunner of the fifth-century Council of 500, to act as a check on the Areopagos. Aristotle and Plutarch agree that he did and modern historians who reject their evidence do so on purely

a priori grounds; that the idea was too advanced for Solon who could not have envisaged anything so 'democratic' in principle as a fifth-century-type Council, that there would be nothing for such a body to do in so primitive a society where the assembly, whose affairs it was supposed to administer, cannot have played a significant enough role to need such control. But when we know nothing of the composition of this Council beyond the fact that *thetes* were excluded from it, nothing of its election or appointment, or of the terms of service, we can hardly assert that it had anything much of fifth-century democracy about it, and if it is argued that its mere existence would be evidence of thinking too advanced for the moderate Solon, the answer, as we have seen, is that Solon was advanced. Again its potential usefulness is demonstrated by the simple fact, ignored by the doubters, that Solon's reforms would have had small chance of success or even of survival when the only permanent organ of state was a still predominantly Eupatrid Areopagos.

When even its existence can be doubted it would be foolish to speculate about the Council's constitutional duties. They can hardly have been onerous. If an early sixth-century building recently revealed in the south-west corner of the Agora was indeed the headquarters of this Council as the excavators reasonably suggest, we must imagine occasional meetings in the open air (the building is too small to seat 40 let alone 400), perhaps once a month (like those of a similar popular body in Ionian Chios only slightly later), to decide (again on the Chian parallel) on what business should be brought before the assembly, perhaps to make recommendations on this business, very probably to arrange for the hearing of legal cases where appeal had been made against a magistrate's verdict or even to hear some of these cases itself. But no more than that. Enough however to provide a focus for resistance to any Eupatrid attempt to ignore or undermine the Solonian settlement.

That such attempts were made and that they centred as we should expect around the elections is clear from the history of the following years. Twice in a decade the word *anarchia* was inscribed on the official list of chief magistrates to indicate that no archon had been elected, a sure sign of trouble; finally in 582 an elected archon, Damasias, remained in office for more than his appointed year, in fact for two years and two months, before he was ejected by force. Damasias was of Eupatrid family but so were some of Solon's supporters – we cannot be sure whether his attempted tyranny was an answer by Eupatrids to the too great success of Solon's measures or a move by Solon's men to win for themselves more than Solon's measures were giving them. Either way it is a mark, if one were needed, that legislation of itself does not solve a crisis.

The solution to the problem of Damasias also gives us the only possible clue to the second problem – how many new men became eligible for highest office under Solon's system. When Damasias was finally ejected, Aristotle says, 'because of the dissension they decided to choose ten archons, five Eupatrids, three "Countrymen" and two "Artisans", to rule for the following year' (*Athenian Constitution*, 13). Whatever the exact significance of this choice (it is unknown), whatever the precise meaning of these castes, the 'Countrymen' and the 'Artisans' (again it is unknown, though, of course, those eligible must have been *hippeis* as well), and whether the defeat of Damasias was a victory for Eupatrids, for Solon's men or a fair compromise between the two, in any case it is likely that the proportions correspond in some degree to the number of candidates available, in other words that the number of non-Eupatrids was at least of the same order as the number of Eupatrids, not more than double, let us say, not less than half.

This figure, rough though it may be, gives us some measure of the change which Solon was trying to bring to Athenian government, just as the violence in the years that followed his reforms shows far more clearly than the reforms themselves not only the resentment of the Eupatrid, faced with the loss of his inherited position, but the hard ambition of the new men, of the large group of new men, who would be satisfied with nothing less than the actual exercise of power. In the case of Korinth and of Sparta we had to guess at their presence behind the revolutions; in Athens, even if we cannot name them or, very clearly, explain their origins we do at least know that they were there. Furthermore we know that in terms of immediate political reality it was they who won in the Solonian revolution. *Hektemoroi*, hoplites, any other discontented groups were merely tools.

Solon and the 'demos'

But even the meanest tool has its price. What price had been paid to other, more ordinary Athenians, to the *zeugitai* (let us call them the hoplites) and the *thetes*, for their support?

Those Athenians who had already been enslaved at home were set free and any who could be found of those who had been sold abroad were brought home. Debtors were freed of their debts. The *hektemoros* too escaped from his annual 'debt' and with it he lost his inferiority. From all of these and many others the possibility of future enslavement was removed by the ban on personal security for debt. The vast majority of those who benefited in these ways would certainly become *thetes*, though there may have been more hoplites than we suspect in need of relief, but it is impossible to guess how large a proportion of the thetic class these new Athenian 'Equals' would make, or how large a proportion of the new *demos* was thetic.

But we can form some pictures of what this new *demos* looked like, whatever its past history. Since Aristotle claims that the rich had owned the land which the *hektemoros* worked and further that Solon did not redistribute land (this with Solon's own words to support him), it has been argued that the freed *hektemoros* automatically lost the fields to which he had been tied, that Solon thus created a large class of landless men who would then continue as hired labourers in the country or find employment in the expanding industry of the city. But this can hardly be true. Later Attika was a country of small farmers, not of large estates and hired labourers – where did these small farms come from? Where did the hired labourers disappear to? Nor can expanding 'industry' account for much – how many potters were there in Athens in 594? as many as 100? There could hardly have been more. Aristotle's belief that the rich owned the land must be either a mistake or a misunderstanding of the *de facto* control which no one would deny that the rich must have had. Indeed the question who had legal title to the *hektemoros*' fields may well be an empty one (above, p. 48), but he and his family had certainly been tied to it for long enough to make it 'his' in sentiment and surely it became 'his' legally when Solon removed the *horoi*, the markers which showed that he and his land together 'belonged' to someone else. Solon's own words imply as much.

. . . the great Mother of the Olympian gods, the black Earth, from whom I once raised the *horoi* that were planted in many places, the Earth that was formerly enslaved and is now set free. (Fragment 36)

The *hektemoros*, then, became a small, independent farmer, like thousands of other small and less small farmers, throughout Attika, and with them made up the bulk of the *demos*; there were besides some fishermen, some traders, some artisans, but certainly not enough of them to affect the basically agricultural colour of the whole, particularly as most of them existed to feed farmers, to serve farmers or to dispose of farmers' goods, and besides would often have some land of their own which would be tended by their wives or children while they looked for extra profit elsewhere. The *demos*, then, was pretty homogeneous in its interests, and in its class. A few extra acres would make hoplites out of *thetes*; they do not make a different kind of man.

In chapter 1, I argued that there was no substantial political difference between these two classes in the fifth century; in a very different way the same, I suspect, was true of the early sixth century. It is possible now as it was not then to see a formal distinction between them – some political offices were open to hoplites *qua* hoplites and one of these, probably the most significant, would be membership of the Council; since it is even likely that they would regularly provide a majority of this Council we must not minimise the influence they may have had in the running of Athens' affairs. But to say that many (or even all) of the lower administrative class were hoplites is not to say that many (still less all) hoplites were willing or able to administer. Political consciousness and political ambition seep down only slowly through the different levels of society; by the late fifth century the line of consciousness was certainly to be drawn well below the hoplite/thetic barrier; at some earlier date, no doubt, it roughly corresponded with this barrier but we have no reason whatsoever to suppose that that point was reached in the time of Solon. Indeed the view that he himself takes of Athenian society tells clearly that it was not:

I gave to the people such recognition as sufficed for it. . . . But those with power . . . (Fragment 5)

The 'people' here must include the hoplite class or at least the vast majority of it and they do not belong to the select body of 'those with power'.

I would guess, then, that no more than a handful of hoplites had either the interest or indeed the resources to take an active part in public life and these few were given the opportunity they wanted. In taking it they ranged themselves, however humbly, with 'those with power' rather than with the mass of their hoplite colleagues. They and the *thetes* stand together on the other side as 'the people', the *demos*.

The rights which the *demos* received under the Solonian constitution are clear and simple; the right to attend and vote in the assembly and the right to serve as members of the new court of appeal, the Heliaia; for *thetes de iure*, for most hoplites *de facto* that was all.

The first, of course, was nothing new; there had been an assembly before Solon (p. 146) and it would be open, no doubt, to all free adult male Athenians. It is conceivable that *hektemoroi* were regarded as sufficiently unfree to be excluded, conceivable though I think unlikely. But even if admitted we may be sure that few, very very few, would attend – the *hektemoros* had more pressing claims on his time than that. Nor indeed is it likely that many of the poor or of the distant would choose to use their rights even after Solon. Xenophanes, the Ionian poet, drew a picture of his native Kolophon not long after Solon's time:

They walked to the assembly, trailing their purple cloaks, not less than a thousand all told, fine-looking men, proud of their well-groomed hair, drenched with the scent of subtle perfumes. (Fragment 3)

The politically active part of Solon's *demos* may have done without some of Kolophon's luxury (Ionians were notorious dandies) but even it did not yet include the great unwashed mass – politics still needed leisure.

But even if the assembly was not created by him or its composition much altered by him, the change he brought to its competence was enormous. Firstly it met by rule not at the whim of magistrate or Areopagos and thus at one stroke it was given an existence of its own, a character of its own. Moreover, however docile it may have been at the start, regular meetings would force on its attention a far greater amount of public business than it could ever before have dreamt existed. Familiarity breeds confidence. Secondly, either by Solonian legislation or accidentally as a result of increasing confidence it came to be taken for granted that decisions, the ultimate decisions on an increasing range of subjects should be taken in the assembly and, possibly by Solonian legislation, decisions were now taken in a way that focused the attention of every member of the assembly on his own personal responsibility – by counting hands. It is much easier to lose oneself in a general shout of 'yes' or 'no' such as satisfied the Spartans than in deliberately raising a hand or casting a vote. Responsibility breeds confidence. Thirdly, again either by accident or Solonian design, the assembly now played a real part in the choice of magistrates. At the most they had previously given formal approval to a choice already made in the Areopagos; whatever the rivalries among the nobles we must suppose that somehow an annual choice 'emerged' as a leader used to 'emerge' for the British Conservative party and, like him, became at once a unanimous choice. But now the division in the potential ruling class was too serious and too basic to allow any such decision to be reached by polite negotiation or quiet manœuvre; whether enforced by Solon or not, the people had a real choice put before them, a choice which varies in significance according to whether we accept sortition or not but still a choice. A further responsibility and, in time, further confidence.

But, of course, we cannot read back these all-important results into Solon's own intentions; even if he did actually legislate on all these points (and I regard that as very doubtful indeed) he cannot have intended to produce the assembly which, ultimately, he did – 'the practitioner of social change' as Aneurin Bevan once said 'knows what he wants to do . . . but he never knows what he is doing until after he has done it' – often long after. Solon could not have conceived of a self-confident mass of ordinary men. The question we must ask is did he want to do *anything* at all for this mass which would surprise or shock the average aristocrat of his day; there is little in the evidence so far discussed to suggest that he did.

But the second right he gave to the *demos* is more revealing. Previously, in so far as there was a state-run legal system, it was administered by Areopagites or at the very least was under the ultimate control of Areopagites. Here Solon introduced two changes which, again, had consequences which he could not have foreseen, but which could not have been made without some element of deliberate intention. He threw it open to any Athenian to institute a prosecution and he created a new non-Areopagite court to hear appeals against the verdict of a magistrate.

Those who dislike Athenian democracy are quick to point out that the first of these was ultimately responsible for the growth of one of the less attractive professions of fifth-century Athens – the professional informer, the *sycophant* who by threat of prosecution under Solon's law could turn an easy blackmailed penny. They do not usually notice that it must also have played its part in producing that very 'conservative' virtue, the almost exaggerated reverence for 'The Laws' as such which is one of the most striking characteristics of the later so-called 'radicals' (below, p. 221). Indeed, Solon's chief concern here would have been, as it so often was, to encourage the development of this feeling; it is very much a part of that de-personalisation of the constitution which is the keynote of the legislation. But in encouraging anyone who wished to share this responsibility Solon may well have realised that he was likely to strike a spark in ordinary men – litigation is more immediately appealing than legislation.

This he 'may well' have realised; he cannot have failed to realise some of the implications of his new court. The exact range of its competence is disputed; the mechanics of its operation unknown but at the very least in some cases an Athenian could appeal against some kinds of punishment imposed by a magistrate and appeal to a jury composed of any of the men who sat in the assembly (at first the jury may well have been the assembly itself; later probably a body selected from it). I am unwilling to imagine that many Athenians took advantage of the opportunity in the first few years or that the jury had the courage to find in the appellant's favour, if any did, but the principle is inescapable and Solon must have been aware of it. Once more the laws are being set above the magistrate who administers them and this time the final judgment on those laws is to be given by a random cross-section of as many Athenians as care to take an interest.

Given such a role for the *demos* in judicial matters it is not un-reasonable to suppose that Solon intended it to have a comparably positive role in politics, in the assembly, but before we are carried away into fantasies about a 'democratic' Solon, it would be as well to look at his own assessment of what he had done. 'I gave to the *demos* as much privilege as was sufficient for it, neither robbing it of honour nor trying to grasp more for it . . .' 'the *demos* will best follow its leaders when it is neither driven by violence nor given too free a rein . . .' 'If one is to give the *demos* a straight rebuke, it is that they could never have even dreamed before of what they now have . . .' These remarks all come from poems written after Solon's archonship (Fragments 5–6 and 37), how long after we do not know. The last is not particularly revealing though it shows clearly enough that the *demos* had soon adjusted itself to its new position and had begun to look still further ahead; it also presents the familiar but always pathetic figure of the old revolutionary who cannot believe that his own revolution was not the ultimate one. But the first two passages show as clearly as we could wish what Solon thought that revolution was. The word I have translated 'privilege' (*geras*) can indeed mean something formal but here I am sure it points far more to the estimation, as it were, of which such formalities are a recognition. Similarly 'honour' (*timê*) may be concrete but here it is much more the 'standing' which attracts the 'honours'. In other words Solon believed that the *demos* should not be trodden underfoot, that it merited a certain amount of recognition and even some tangible 'privileges' based on that recognition – but, as every recruit to the army knows, even a formal privilege is not a right. Besides, what is given is 'sufficient' – sufficient for what? Sufficient presumably to produce the perfect society outlined in the second passage, a society in which the *demos* obeys its leaders. Again we think of the army. There is an officer class, 'those with power', and there are 'other ranks'. Like the good aristocrat or the good general, Solon likes to think that his troops are happy; he goes further – he thinks that they should be happy, almost that they have a right to be happy, but he is far from realising that they might possibly have a say in deciding what happiness is or even take a hand in leading themselves towards it.

7 Tyranny in Athens

Solon's 'failure'

Solon tried to modernise Athens without a revolution. By legislation he removed what he thought was wrong and created a constitution in which every section of society had what seemed to him at the time its rightful place, and which would be, he hoped, sufficiently flexible to adjust itself to future changes without the need for violence; above all he had done everything in his power to ensure that Athenians would come to regard this constitution as sacred, to change it perhaps, but always to change it from within. For Solon himself I am sure that this was both the most essential and the most progressive aspect of his work. He had strong progressive views on other things as well, on the role of the *demos* in the state among them, but he would have been astonished at the time we spend searching through his measures or his poems for the slightest clue to the extent of his 'democratic' intentions, while scarcely noticing this fundamental belief in the importance of law, any kind of law, as such.

Solon was not primarily a democrat or a moderate democrat or an oligarch, he was a constitutionalist and his determination to convert Athenians to his way of thinking is seen throughout his work. The magistrate was to be the servant of the law, not its master – each one had to swear that he would dedicate a golden statue to the gods if he failed to observe the rules – and the people were there to see that he was an obedient servant – hence the court of appeal. Nor was the general responsibility left collective and therefore vague – every individual had the right to take legal action on behalf of another and, to us a curious rule, had the duty to take part in any civil strife that might arise, surely a sign of Solon's belief that the majority would always favour law and order but, a shrewd thought, might have to be prodded into defending it. After his legislation, which was to be left unchanged for a hundred years, he himself left Athens for ten, making the people swear to make no changes in his absence – even this is part of the same pattern. Aristotle gives the reason (*Athenian Constitution*, 11): 'He did not wish to have to interpret the laws himself but wanted everyone to act according to what was written,' i.e. he did not want it to be 'Solon's code', depending on him for its authority and perhaps for its survival, he wanted it to be 'The Code'.

But only thirty-four years after he had fashioned it, in 561 BC, Peisistratos set himself outside the constitution and became tyrant. Peisistratos, whose mother was Solon's mother's niece, had grown up in the Solonian circle. He would have been too young to join in the struggle which led to 594 but in the years thereafter he won popular glory as a highly successful general (he captured the Megarian port of Nisaia for Athens) and, no doubt, Solon's increasing disapproval as a radical, rather too radical politician. At some point he went too far, the Solonian 'party' split and Peisistratos emerged as the leader of a new 'left wing'. As such he appeared one day wounded in the *agora*, victim, he claimed, of an opposition plot; the people believed him in spite of the warnings of a now aged Solon and voted him a bodyguard. But Solon was right; Peisistratos used the bodyguard to seize the Akropolis. It is easy to say that Solon had failed not in 561 but in 594; in a sense he had. But it is far less easy to see where he had failed and almost impossible to think that he could have succeeded.

The natural conclusion from Peisistratos' 'radicalism' would be that Solon failed because he had not gone far enough and, since it is possible to argue, though wrongly I think, that the core of Peisistratos' support was the agricultural poor, many have believed that the failure lay principally in the economic field, that the *hektemoroi* though technically freed had not been helped to make an adequate living and so turned to Peisistratos for more drastic remedy. Others have preferred to point to the continuous struggles over the archonship in the years after Solon and to argue that the Eupatrids had retained too great an advantage in the political system; that violence was needed to break their hold. There is much truth in this and there may be some, though very much less, in the economic answer, but neither, I think, gives nearly enough weight to one vital factor, the development of Athens between 594 and 561; both ignore the possibility that Peisistratos may have came to power not because Solon in some respect or other had done too little but because in others he had succeeded all too well.

Before 600 BC, as we have seen, some Athenian pottery was reaching the approaches to the Black Sea; some too has been found in Italy and even in southern France. But the quantity is tiny. In the next half century, however, there is hardly a site throughout the Mediterranean or Black Sea which has not produced evidence of the beginning and the rapid intensification of trade in Athenian goods. Solon did not begin the process but there is no doubt that he both understood it and deliberately encouraged it; foreign crafts-men were welcomed in Athens, native Athenians exhorted to learn a trade, the production of oil was forced on anyone who wished to sell abroad by banning the export of any other natural produce, access to the sea made safe by the capture of the island of Salamis which fronted Athens' port at Phaleron, exchange of goods in a wider or more profitable area made easier by a change in the stan-dard of weights and measures; all this by legislation or direct action. At the same time the great political achievement of 594 can hardly have failed to lift Athenian morale, to help in setting free the energy which by 560 had turned Athens into a substantial commercial city, modest still by comparison with Korinth or Aigina but very far removed from her depressed seventh-century self.

This extraordinary expansion was not all Solon's work, but his deliberate contribution to it is far from insignificant. In turn there is no positive evidence to connect this expansion with the rise of Peisistratos but common sense would suggest some sort of link. If there was it was Solon's success far more than his failure that mat-tered, for in the first place it is not very easy to believe that any great number of poor ex-*hektemoroi* starved their way through thirty years of boom or, if they did, that they had the strength left at the end of it to shout hurrah for Peisistratos. Poor farmers there were, now and always in Attika, the majority of them, perhaps, living in those parts of eastern Attika from which Peisistratos drew much of his support; no doubt they stood solidly behind him for

A lifesize male figure in marble (a *kouros*) from Anavyssos in SE Attika.
It probably comes from an aristocratic family cemetery, and may well
represent an Alkmeonid killed at Pallene. An inscription below reads:
'Stop and grieve at the tomb of Kroisos, killed . . . in the front rank of battle'
Kroisos will have been named after the King of Lydia with whom
Alkmeonids had close connections.

they were rewarded when he was in power. But secondly, in an
economy expanding as rapidly as this, the successful must be
stronger than the failures and it is to them that we look for effective
discontent, to the potter who could now afford a slave, to the
hektemoros who became a potter, to the farmer, ex-*hektemoros* or
not, whose newly planted olives were beginning to pay off, to all
those who now had time to give a thought to politics.

That they had not only the time but the inclination may also be
Solon's doing. Thirty years will not turn a serf into a democrat, but
it is long enough to give men some understanding of what they have
already been given, long enough to let them begin to feel their way
towards a vote against authority in the assembly, towards rejecting
a magistrate's decision in the courts. It is worth remembering that
in 561 BC only men over fifty could have had any real memory of
political life before Solon; the rest had grown up to take both
assembly and courts for granted. It was a vote of the assembly
which gave Peisistratos the bodyguard with which he seized the
Akropolis and began his tyranny. In other words, thanks to Solon,
Athens had been transformed economically and politically and it is
at least as possible that the explanation of Peisistratos' tyranny lies
in new stresses developed by the new situation as that it is to be
found in some long-standing weakness which Solon had overlooked.

A clue to the nature of these stresses might be found in the split
among the Solonians which produced on the one hand the faction
of the SW. coast – the *Paralioi* – led by the Alkmeonids, and that of
the *Hyperakrioi*, the men beyond the hills, Peisistratos' followers,
but there is nothing in the evidence to explain it. Economically there
is no great difference between the two areas, and, although the
famous silver mines of Laurion, a vital source of Athens' later
wealth, lay for the most part in Peisistratos' territory, there is no
good reason to think that they were yet being exploited sufficiently
to produce any dramatic effect on the pattern of regional differ-
erences. It is true that Peisistratos himself developed interests in the
rich mining area of southern Thrace during one of his periods of
exile; true also that coinage was introduced for the first time to

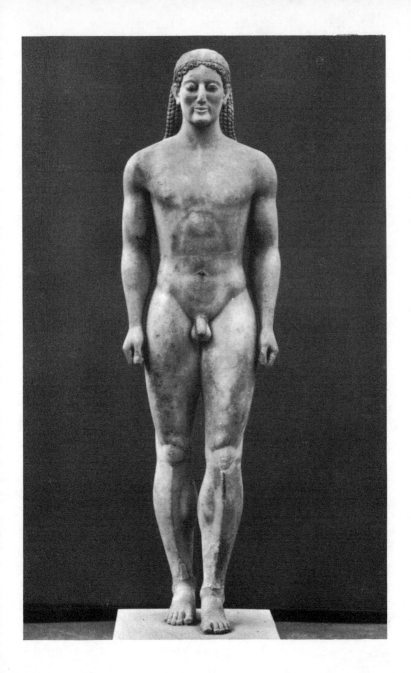

Athens very shortly before he came to power and that the superb Athenian 'Owls', later to become the most popular coinage in the east Mediterranean, were first struck during the tyranny. In other words a connection is not impossible but it would be rash to affirm it without better evidence than we have.

Politically it is equally difficult to see any certain distinction between the two. In the fifteen years after 560 Peisistratos was twice exiled and twice returned to power. Soon after the *coup* of 561 the leaders of the Coast and the Plain, Megakles the Alkmeonid and a certain Lykourgos, forgot their own differences for long enough to chase Peisistratos out of Athens. But at once they fell to squabbling again and Megakles himself helped to engineer Peisistratos' return. A fine-looking girl from the countryside, dressed up to look like the goddess Athena, rode beside Peisistratos on his chariot and the word was passed round that the goddess herself was bringing back her favourite. Lykourgos could not compete.

To mark the new alliance Peisistratos then married Megakles' daughter but, already equipped with sons by other wives, he had no desire to link himself too closely with the Alkmeonids, still officially under Delphi's curse for their part in the Kylonian affair, and the poor girl did not find in marriage all that she had expected. She told her mother who told her father and Peisistratos found it politic to withdraw again to safety abroad where he spent some ten years of exile before, in rather more serious mood, he landed in Attika with an army and fought his way back (at the battle of Pallene in 546), this time to unchallenged control. In the political manœuvrings and realignments of these years it seems that the Coast did stand in some way between the two extremes of Plain and Hill, i.e. there was something more involved in the quarrel than mere personal or local faction. Possibly the *Hyperakrioi* found it more difficult than the Coast to exploit the chance that Solon had given them (for reasons of distance or whatever) so that the latter, half-accepted by the old Eupatrids of the Plain, lost interest in carrying on the fight for others. But again there is no evidence.

In other words the reasons for Athens' rejection of the Solonian solution are, except in broadest outline, lost. It may be that Solon underestimated Eupatrid tenacity and overestimated the open-mindedness of those whom he most immediately benefited but that is the limit of his error and if he did it is difficult to see what he could have done about it short of that violence which he most wanted to avoid. Beyond that we can only say that the extraordinary economic expansion of these years had so upset the pattern on which Solon worked, that the machinery of constitutional government which he devised did so much to develop the political consciousness of less exalted Athenians, that a sufficient number of them, whether to press this expansion yet further in the same or perhaps in new directions, or to give some kind of expression to the consciousness which that machinery could not give, were prepared to abandon for a time the basic principle on which Solon had tried to rely in creating both.

The tyranny and prosperity

Curiously enough, however, by abandoning the principle, by accepting the unconstitutional rule of Peisistratos and, after his death in 528, that of his son Hippias, the Athenians did not do anything to hold up the development of their political consciousness. Three factors contributed, still more prosperity, more 'democracy' and more centralisation. All of these natural continuations of processes begun before, but all given added impetus by the tyrants.

Peisistratos' accession seems to have brought a substantial change in Athenian foreign policy; new friends were acquired, some old ones perhaps lost. The result, very broadly, a much closer relationship with the islands of the Aegean and with Argos. But this had no effect as far as we can see on the general direction of economic growth nor on its intensity; the potters carried black-figure painting to its finest point after the middle of the century and about 530 began to experiment with the new and potentially even finer red-figure style; a ten per cent tax was levied on the produce of the land but some, at least, of the revenue was used to help the poorer farmers; and the potters' vases and the farmers' oil went out in increasing quantities to every available market; the details of these and other developments do not concern us (the coinage, an extensive building programme, a colony on the Hellespont to secure the Black Sea grain route); it is enough to note that later Athenians looked back on Peisistratos' rule as a golden age; that during it, for more and more, life became something other than a desperate struggle to survive.

The tyranny and 'democracy'

Nor was it only after the expulsion of Peisistratos' son, Hippias, that ordinary men could use their leisure to continue the lessons in democracy that Solon's constitutional machinery had offered them. Peisistratos made few if any substantial changes in the system and although at the highest level the mere existence of a tyrant robbed politics of any meaning, only the nobility, new and old, were likely to feel the loss – 'the tyrants', says Thucydides 'observed the existing laws; only they saw to it that the highest offices were always held by their own friends'. In other words those parts of the machine which lesser men might use or even operate functioned as before – the courts, the assembly and the Council. Indeed there are even signs that Peisistratos encouraged them. Solon's popular court, the Heliaia, was not, as far as we know provided with any material equipment, but in the fifth century and later the democratic juries which developed from the Heliaia met in and around one and later two or three porticos which filled the southern side of the Agora. Abutting on the earliest of these porticos is a simple rectangular structure of stone which, the excavators have plausibly guessed, was the first permanent home for the Heliaia. It probably dates from the early years of the tyranny. Again the fifth-century Council was provided with two buildings – a meeting-house and record office and a residence for the standing-committee; the first was built about 500 as a successor to the tiny house which probably served as headquarters for Solon's Council;

the other about 470, it too on the ruins of an earlier structure but one for which it seems that Peisistratos, not Solon, was responsible.

One of the motives behind the provision of these two public offices was no doubt the same as that behind the rest of the tyrants' extensive building schemes – the glorification of Athens; but they cannot have failed to enhance the prestige of the bodies who now occupied them nor is it likely that the enhancement was entirely accidental. Indeed it is worth noting that the existence of a residence for the Council, although not implying the introduction as yet of anything resembling the fifth-century committee system would seem to suggest that its members were now in action or on call for periods long enough to make them tired or hungry. Perhaps this was already the case before 560; but equally it may be partly Peisistratos' doing. Moreover an active Council should imply an active assembly and although there is something obviously unreal in the marriage of a supposedly free assembly with a dictatorial régime, the unreality is not necessarily obvious to those who take part, given always that the régime has their sympathy, and that they have never had a proper taste of absolute power. The French parliamentarian may regret the Fourth Republic but the average Russian is quite happy with his Soviet and has not shown much longing for the days of the Tsar.

The tyranny and centralisation

The increased centralisation of the government which Peisistratos brought must also have tended to increase both the importance and the self-importance of these central institutions but this, by far the most striking achievement of the tyranny, is more significant for its general effect on the morale of ordinary Athenians than for any formal strengthening of the state administration. In concentrating as we naturally do on this administration it is easy to lose sight of the fact that it cannot have played any very great part in the life or thoughts of the great majority of the Athenian population, scattered as they still were in the small villages and townships of the

An Attic black-figure *kyathos* (a cup
with a single high handle) of
the later sixth century, when red-figure
technique was already beginning to predominate.
The scene shows a dead man with attendant
mourners, male on left, female on right.

Attic countryside. For them the affairs of Marathon, Sounion or
Acharnai bulked far larger than those of Athens, and those affairs
remained by and large in the hands of the men who had always
held them, the local aristocratic family, the leaders of the clans and
phratries. In so far as this control had depended on the inherited
acquiescence of the ruled it must have been seriously weakened in
the general assault on the aristocracy of the preceding century and
in particular by the ending of the formal bond of hektemorage but,

An Attic red-figure cup, showing a battle-scene. The date is about 510 BC; the artist Oltos, one of the first great names in red-figure. His style is robust and misses some of the delicacy that the new technique made possible but he has a good command of design and adapts his scenes admirably to the space and contour of the vase.

no doubt, a considerable residue remained; it was not in the interest of the new post-Solonian politician to destroy his own traditional following. Besides their hold was not only sentimental; the whole of local life and local administration, as we have seen, had grown up inside and around the phratry system and Solon had done nothing, as far as we know, to make any substantial alteration.

Nor was Peisistratos' formal contribution very considerable. He instituted a board of itinerant judges and it is a reasonable guess that they were intended to take away at least some of the legal authority that remained in phratry hands. But beyond that nothing. Informally, however, the story is very different.

It is not recorded that any of Peisistratos' enemies suffered in the comic-opera intrigues of 560–556. But in the fighting of 546 some of his opponents of the Coast or Plain were killed, many others must have fled the country. Absence may make the heart grow fonder but it also interferes with practice in the techniques of fondness and many an Athenian must have noticed for the first time after 546 that life could go on successfully even when the local manor was deserted and, in the years that followed, must have gradually forgotten how he had behaved when the manor was full. Even where the local aristocrat had survived the crisis, a difference would be felt. Of old when he had set off to 'represent' his followers in the national government he had been swallowed up in the confused intriguing factions of the capital and, if successful, had re-emerged as a man who had taken on a crowd of equals and defeated them. Now, at best, he returned as a man who had persuaded the undisputed master, Peisistratos; an intermediary, not a champion.

Thus far the effects were accidental. But the tyrants did everything in their power deliberately to encourage the subordination of the local to the national, that is of the aristocratic to their own private interest, this not by any positive interference with the former but by very positive encouragement of the latter. Their treatment of the coinage is symptomatic. The chronology and much else about early Athenian coins is obscure but it is at least certain that the first self-consciously national issue was produced during the tyranny, carrying on one face the head of Athens' particular goddess Athena and on the other Athena's symbol the owl. In the field of religion too national cults and festivals were fostered in a way that must have drawn men's attention and devotion from the local shrine of the family or the phratry. Athena again was one of the main beneficiaries; a new home was built for her on the Akropolis and the great four-yearly festival in her honour, the Panathenaia, instituted shortly before the tyranny, became the central event in

An Athenian silver tetradrachm (four-drachma piece) of about 510 BC. The first 'Owls', as they were called, were minted under Hippias and, thanks to their purity and reliability, soon became the most popular coinage in the Mediterranean. In the later fifth century this coin would have represented about four days' pay for a skilled worker, twelve (after 425 eight) days' pay for jury-service.

An Aiginetan 'Turtle'. Athens coined for some thirty years before using a national symbol. Aigina, the first mainland state to found a mint, from the start (about 600 BC or shortly before) adopted the turtle. At first elegance was confined to the obverse, the reverse (as here) showed merely an incuse mark, i.e. that of the ground on which the coin was stamped.

A Korinthian 'Pegasos'. Korinth which began coining at or about the time of the fall of the tyranny (582 BC), with its colonies, used the winged horse Pegasos as its symbol. A distinguishing letter (here the archaic *koppa* for Korinth) marked the issuing city. The incuse is now beginning to acquire some degree of self-conscious design.

An Attic black-figure amphora of about 560 BC, one of the earliest 'Panathenaic amphoras', i.e. vases produced to be filled with olive-oil as prizes at the Panathenaic games. One side carried a portrait of Athena, the other often an athletic scene, here a racing-chariot. The workmanship, as here, often fell far short of the best.

Athens' religious calendar. An annual festival was created in honour of Dionysos, the Dionysia, which provided several days of musical and primitive dramatic contests from which Athenian comedy and tragedy were to develop. The more spiritual cult of Demeter was honoured by a new Hall of Initiation at Eleusis and a fine sanctuary at the SE. corner of the Agora in Athens. The list could be extended. The priesthoods in these national cults were still in the hands of aristocrats – those of Demeter, for example, were, and always remained, the property of two great families, the Eumolpidai and the Kerukes – but they were aristocrats acting for Athens not merely for their own personal following.

In these and many other ways Athenians were made conscious of their nationality; the idea of citizenship, fully but to some extent only theoretically defined by Solon, acquired another element of real meaning. The man from Marathon was still very much a Marathonian but increasingly he was acquiring non-Marathonian interests and as he did so he became slowly aware that he belonged to a much larger body, the Athenian *demos*, aware too that he had more in common with his like in Sounion or Acharnai than with any local aristocracy.

Replicas of statues of Harmodios and Aristogeiton by Kritios and Nesiotes, set up in the Agora in 477 BC to replace an earlier work stolen by the Persians in 480. Earlier reconstructions have placed the two heroes back to back. The present photograph attempts artificially to show how they would appear in a new and almost certainly correct pose suggested by Mr B. B. Shefton.

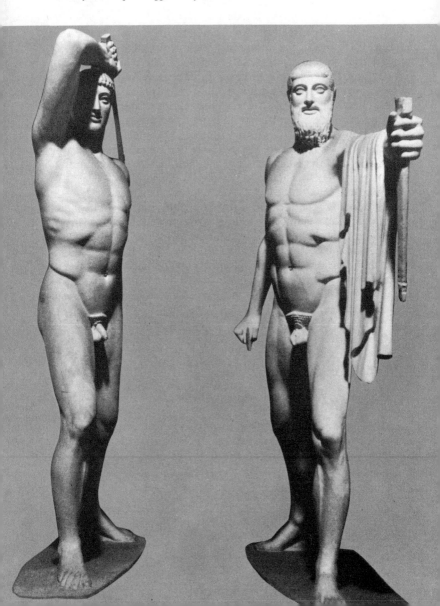

8 The reforms of Kleisthenes

The expulsion of Hippias

When Peisistratos died in 528 the tyranny passed to his eldest son Hippias who ruled not quite so confidently as his father but still securely, for the next fourteen years. Then a quarrel with two of his supporters, Harmodios and Aristogeiton, led to the assassination of Hippias' brother, Hipparchos, and to three final years of suspicion and brutality. The Alkmeonids both before and during the tyranny had now collaborated, now quarrelled with the tyrants, but at the time of Hipparchos' murder they found themselves in exile once more and decided to use the unrest to secure their return. A direct attempt at unassisted invasion failed but then, through the intervention of the Delphic oracle, they won the help of Sparta and, in 510 BC, with a Spartan army behind, or perhaps rather in front of them, they re-entered Attika to drive out Hippias and his family. Many other aristocrats had been in exile; others had at some point made their peace and returned to Athens; others again had stayed in the city throughout. All alike now thought that they could take up the game of faction politics where they had left it for the last time in 546, take it up and play it with the old weapons and by the old rules. By 508 they had resolved themselves into two main groups, one led by Kleisthenes the Alkmeonid, the other by one Isagoras, two aristocratic groups of just that sort which Peisistratos had had to contend with in 561. These two men, Herodotos says (*v.* 66), *edunasteuon*, were 'dynasts', and the word is as clear a sign as we could want of the kind of politics they played – each 'stood at the head of an aristocratic pyramid'. But Kleisthenes found himself defeated and, to save himself, Herodotos goes on, 'added the *demos* to his faction', a *demos* 'which he had previously ignored'. Herodotos may not have chosen his words deliberately but they could not be more apt. 'Faction' is again an aristocratic term; it belongs in a world in which a *demos* does not exist as a political entity, in which a *demos* cannot play any part. Like Herodotos, I believe, Kleisthenes mixed his categories with disastrous results – for himself and his kind.

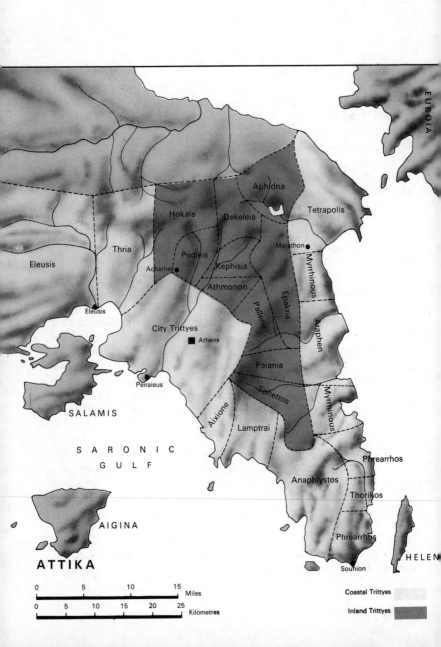

EUBOIA

Aphidna

Hokale   Dekeleia   Tetrapolis

Thria   Pedieis   Marathon

Eleusis   Acharnai   Kephisia

Eleusis   Athmonon   Myrrhinous

City Trittyes   Pallene   Epakria   Araphen

■ Athens

Paiania   Myrrhinous

Peiraieus   Sphettos

SALAMIS   Aixone   Lamptrai   Phrearrhos

S A R O N I C   Anaphlystos

G U L F   Thorikos

AIGINA   Phrearrhos   HELEN

ATTIKA   Sounion

| 0 | | 5 | | 10 | | 15 | Miles |
| 0 | 5 | 10 | 15 | 20 | 25 | Kilometres |

Coastal Trittyes

Inland Trittyes

This map is based on that of C. W. J. Eliot, *The Coastal Demes of Attika* (p. 139). The names of the *trittyes* (literally 'thirds' of the local tribes) are often uncertain. The exact boundaries of the city *trittyes* are also as yet obscure.

Examples of continuous inland and coastal *trittyes* are: Tetrapolis and Aphidna; Araphen and Epakria; Thorikos and Sphettos (?). Myrrhinous and Phrearrhos (north), on the east coast, are examples of divided *trittyes* (another is in the city area).

What was probably the Alkmeonid family cemetery (from which came the statue, page 179) has been discovered in the sw coastal *trittys*, Anaphlystos; it was attached to the city *trittys* of Alopeke, due east of Athens between Tourkovouno and Hymettos (see page 151). It is even possible that the inland *trittys* of this same tribe (Pallene) should be slightly redrawn to make it march fully with Alopeke. In that case another 'natural' Alkmeonid area would have been catered for in the new organisation.

It is worth repeating that these three areas did not correspond with the old 'party' divisions of Plain, Coast and Beyond the Hills (page 158–9). There is some dispute about their exact boundaries but the Plain at least included most if not all of the city *trittyes*, and of the inland *trittyes*, Hecale, Pedieis, Athmonon, Kephisia and Pallene; the Coast was certainly limited to Aixone, Lamptrai, Anaphlystos, Phrearrhos (south); the part Beyond the Hills certainly included Tetrapolis, Aphidna, Araphen, Myrrhinous, Thorikos, and Phrearrhos (north). Doubt mainly centres on the allegiance of the area made up by Paiania and Sphettos. Much respectable modern opinion would assign this to the Hyperakria on the grounds that it is 'beyond' Hymettos. I find the high ground which stretches unevenly from the southern slopes of Pentelikon in an arc round towards Sounion an equally effective barrier and should much prefer to combine the area inside it with the Plain, admittedly only on the *a priori* ground that its richness is likely to have produced an aristocracy quite as well established as that of the central plain.

The new tribal system

But to see more clearly what he was trying to do and where he went wrong we must examine in some detail his actual measures when finally, with the *demos*' firm support, he was able to rout Isagoras together with a Spartan force which Isagoras had summoned in the crisis and to put into effect the proposals with which that support had presumably been won (in 508 BC). On paper it is not a very stunning achievement. The basic administrative unit of Attika became the 'deme', a village, a locality, a ward of the city; the demes, perhaps about 170 in all, were then combined into thirty groups called *trittyes*, one consisting of only one large deme, others of up to ten or so smaller ones, most forming continuous and naturally distinct blocks of territory, a few including one deme which was geographically set apart. Three *trittyes* were then assigned to each of ten new tribes, replacing the four Ionian tribes, one *trittys* chosen, the tradition says by lot, from a group of ten around the city, another from ten along the coast, the third from ten inland. There were certain administrative consequences, the Council now numbered 500, fifty from each tribe, in place of the Solonian 400, there were ten not four tribal commanders, and so on, but none of these seems especially significant. It has been guessed, very plausibly, that more substantial changes were made, in the competence of the Council or of the assembly and in other things, but there is no escaping from the fact that later Athenians remembered of Kleisthenes no more than his tribal reform and the law of ostracism which we shall discuss later. At first sight it is far from easy to see why the *demos* should find this so memorable or at the time so attractive or how it could be said that by it Kleisthenes created Athenian democracy.

Even Aristotle was puzzled and consequently introduced a theory which has been received by later historians with far too much respect; that Peisistratos had given citizenship to a host of immigrants who were disfranchised by the returning aristocrats in 510 and formed the nucleus of Kleisthenes' support; the tribal changes were then introduced to mix up the citizen body and conceal the re-enfranchisement of this support. The facts of disfranchisement and re-enfranchisement behind this theory may well be true but it is, I think, enough to point·out that the disfranchised, however numerous, can hardly have outnumbered the native Athenians, even in the area round the city, and, more important still, that they could not have had what Kleisthenes most needed before his final success, namely votes. Aristotle went so far as to argue that the later official designation of Athenians by name and deme rather than by name and patronymic was introduced by Kleisthenes so that the foreign origin of his new friends should not be revealed as it would be if, in normal Greek practice, they added their fathers' name to their own. Aristotle here hardly gives due credit either to the force of natural curiosity, or to the information service that any small community can offer about any of its members, nor indeed does he explain why a father's name should always reveal what a man's own name could conceal.

The importance of the deme

But the introduction of the deme-name does in fact give a clue to an understanding of one vital element in the reform. It could have only one effect, not to conceal but to emphasise two things, the unity of the deme and the equality of all its members *qua* members, and it is here, in the new status and the internal organisation of the deme that we have, I am sure, the carrot which Kleisthenes dangled before the nose of the Athenian *demos*. Local loyalty is universal: in Attika it had until recently meant everything and still meant much. The deme gave this loyalty a new focus: a deme constitution took the place of phratry practice, deme officials replaced the leading family of the district, and this constitution, moreover, was democratic, the officials were elected.

The phratry, I have argued, was a natural growth of the dis-ordered post-invasion period when a state organisation barely existed. By the sixth century there was such an organisation and it must have spread down to a local level in all manner of different ways – for taxation, for military service and the rest – but, although the details are completely lost to us, it can hardly be doubted that in every department the administration was more or less closely married to the phratry system. To take only one example: without exploring the complications raised by the existence of various subordinate groups it is safe to say that in 510, for the vast majority if not for all Athenians, the necessary and sufficient condition for citizenship was membership of a phratry. Details of the later system are also hard to come by but again it is certain that all these same offshoots of the administration were now channelled through the deme. To continue the example, a citizen was now a man who had been accepted by his demesmen as a true member of the deme.

Annually the deme assembly chose its *demarchos*, its mayor, a council, and other officers, and on this organisation the citizen depended not only for local government as such, but as a source of any direction he received from the national government in Athens and even as the means by which he could acquire not only the training for but even admission to that national government himself. As a member of the Athenian assembly, of course, he was an individual unconnected with any group, but if he became a member of the Athenian Council he did so as a member of his deme. In other words to the mass of Athenians the deme was everything; even to the politically ambitious it could be a useful school and remained a necessary background.

This is not to say that deme democracy was born overnight. No doubt in the early years the *demarchos* was, as often as not, the phratry boss with a different title but the squire is less effective in the Council chamber than in the manor, if only because he has been put there by vote not by birth. And besides, these changes, drastic as they were, were no more than a continuation and formalisation of precisely that process of informal liberation from the shackles of aristocratic control which the tyranny had encouraged. It need not have been very long before the ordinary demesman began to see in the deme name he shared with his aristocratic neighbour, in the deme assembly where he still may have voted for his aristocratic neighbour, real signs of independence and of equality.

The significance of the tribes

But Kleisthenes did more than create the deme; he fitted it into a wider context. He could easily have achieved all the effects noted above without the remarkable superstructure of *trittyes* and tribes which he erected on the deme foundation. Why then create it; why not simply divide the demes regionally among as many tribes as he wished to have and leave it at that? Obviously he wanted either to keep some people apart or to put others together. But why? Broadly speaking there are two possible answers. Either his conversion to the side of the *demos* was genuine and all his measures were designed to safeguard its future (or simply to improve the mechanics of Athenian government) or, while giving the *demos* what it wanted, he tried at the same time to ensure a safe position in the new régime for himself and his family. In the first case the *trittys* system would be designed by combination or separation to remove certain dangers to the internal peace of Attika. In the second the same method would be used to remove or weaken opposition to the Alkmeonids as a family. If we put the problem like this it is obvious that only a very detailed knowledge both of the precise boundaries of a *trittys* and of the economic, social and other patterns in the distribution of the Athenian population could provide a definite answer. We have neither and what follows therefore is largely guesswork. The obvious starting point is the general division of the *trittyes* into their three groups, urban, coastal and inland, but I see no clear explanation of it. Certainly it had nothing to do with the old pre-tyranny parties of Plain, Coast and Hills since the urban distinction is something entirely new and the coastal *trittyes* covered a much larger area than the former *Paralia*, including much of the *Hyperakria*. Nor is it possible to argue with any confidence that Kleisthenes was trying to make each tribe representative of the whole population of Attika; so many fishermen, so many artisans, so many farmers or anything like that. For in this respect the names are misleading – very many, possibly even a majority of the 'urban' population would be farmers, for the urban *trittyes* covered an area which stretched about five miles in each direction from the city itself; a majority of the 'coastal' population would be equally agricultural. Most of the best agricultural land was indeed inland and there may have been other substantial differences between the areas but it is not easy to see what they may have been or to believe that anything of this sort constituted a major motive for the scheme. Besides, in one or two cases, the inland and coastal *trittyes* of the same tribe are contiguous or very nearly contiguous, and, although our ignorance of detail forbids any firm inference from this, one cannot help thinking that putting people together is not the best way of keeping them apart.

This same thought is bound to affect our approach to the next area of speculation, that of the *trittyes* regarded as units rather than as parts of the three groups, bound to suggest, in fact, that the scheme was designed not for any general separation or combination but for separation and/or combination in certain specific cases, that Kleisthenes drew his lines not on any general principle but for particular reasons in particular cases, and a recent study of some of these cases gives the idea some plausibility. The argument starts from the examples, already mentioned, of divided *trittyes*. In at least two cases it is certain that the pockets of territory containing one deme which have been attached to a comparatively distant and certainly geographically distinct *trittys* were the centres of important local cults, of cults, that is, which would previously have been dominated by the great family of the district in question and which would have attracted clients from a much wider area than the deme itself. Under the new rules the cult, as a cult, would still maintain its hold but many of those it affected would belong, politically, to an entirely different unit than those who controlled it; in matters other than religious the great family would have to influence not their old followers from the neighbourhood but a crowd of strangers from over the hill.

The examples of this careful manipulation of the boundaries are very few, but enough to encourage the suspicion that in many other cases as well Kleisthenes divided his *trittys* with the very deliberate intention of breaking up as far as he could the existing pattern of aristocratic influence. There are too many imponderables for us to be able to assess the effects of all this in any detail. Above all we do not know enough of what a *trittys* did as a *trittys* or what a tribe did as a tribe. At one extreme it is certain that neither *trittys* nor tribe meant anything in the national Assembly – there each man was on his own, susceptible to any influence that might be brought to bear on him as an individual, including any hangover there might be of the old obedience to his master's order. To the Athenian in his Assembly Kleisthenes meant nothing. But at the other extreme it is equally certain that either as a soldier or as a member of the national Council he could not escape from tribal or *trittys* influence and the mere fact that his former master now commanded a different regiment, was represented by a different tribal committee in the Council, must have transformed the feelings that he once had had for him. Between the extremes there may have been many other ways, formal and informal, in which he found himself set free from the often indefinable bonds of the phratry-atmosphere.

But *cui bono*? Or better, who suffered? Aristocrats as a body or selected aristocrats? More specifically, did Kleisthenes treat his own family as he treated others? Here there is even more room for doubt but there are two coincidences which raise the suspicion that the Alkmeonids rather than democracy were meant to benefit. Alkmeonids no longer lived in one spot in 508. Their original home had probably been on the SW. coast, in the post-Solonian *Paralia*; now branches of the family were settled in three different demes of the urban area, assigned by Kleisthenes to three different *trittyes*. Another family, who were close to them at the time occupied a fourth deme, part of a fourth *trittys*. Oddly enough these four urban *trittyes* were attached to just those four coastal *trittyes* which together covered the SW. coast, the old *Paralia* which Alkmeonids had once controlled, while the urban *trittys* in which the headquarters

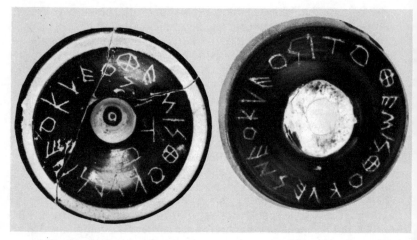

of the family now were was joined to the coastal *trittys* in which their country home had formerly been (and presumably still was).

If this is chance, as it well may be, Kleisthenes by careful planning tried to destroy existing loyalties in order to give his new constitution a chance to grow up before, like the Solonian, it was choked by the too great strength of in-built aristocratic control. If it is not coincidence, Kleisthenes gave the *demos* what they wanted but took good care to see that, while his rivals lost their chance to play the aristocratic game, he and his family kept theirs, indeed increased it by building his own areas of support into the system much as the old aristocrats had theirs enshrined in the phratry-network. In view of Kleisthenes' past history, of his recorded motives for his actions, and of the future history of his family (they are not distinguished for any love they show towards the results of their ancestor's work), I am sure that the second answer is correct, but no one can prove that Kleisthenes was anything but a man who was genuinely converted to a new ideal by his temporary defeat at the hands of Isagoras. As such he would be a rare specimen but not unique.

An *ostrakon* of Aristeides, 'son of Lysimachos' (page 219). Aristeides was ostracised in 482 after a disagreement with Themistokles on the use of a new vein of silver found at Laurion in SE Attika. Aristeides favoured a distribution of the profits, Themistokles the building of the ships which won Salamis (page 204). The Athenians voted for Themistokles, showing once more that democracy need not be either selfish or irresponsible. But Themistokles and Aristeides were not always in different political camps (page 219).

Ostracism

Indeed the idea that Kleisthenes was a disinterested reformer is at first sight made slightly more probable by his introduction of ostracism. By this curious procedure the Athenian *demos* was allowed, once a year if it chose, to send into exile for ten years any one citizen it wished. First a vote was taken to decide whether or not an ostracism was needed; then, if it was, each man scratched on a fragment of pottery (an *ostrakon*) the name of the politician he felt he could best do without; the winner, as it were, left the country.

The first ostracism we know of took place in 487 BC and some historians, worried by the gap of twenty years, have refused to follow our only coherent source on the subject, Aristotle (*Athenian Constitution*, 22), in ascribing its introduction to Kleisthenes; with more reason they have also rejected Aristotle's explanation of it as a safeguard against any future tyranny, pointing out that neither of a tyrant's usual roads to power, force or personal popularity, would be blocked by it. Rather we must see it, I think (though many other theories have been advanced), as giving Athenians a chance to decide on a major issue of policy with absolute finality where indecision might be dangerous or where feelings ran so high that civil strife might result; in short to deal by constitutional means with just that kind of opposition which had existed between Kleisthenes and Isagoras. In that case a Kleisthenic origin need not be doubted.

But does a man who is only out to secure his own position in the state by giving away, presumably, as little as possible to the *demos* and, at the same time, by rigging the system to suit himself, run the risk of putting a weapon like this, a weapon that could easily be turned against him, into the hands of a popular assembly? Does it not rather suggest a man who is planning a peaceful, settled, democratic future for his country? Indeed it does, but the impression may be misleading. Everything depends on how Kleisthenes saw this *demos* which he was 'adding to his faction'. The *demos* itself I have tried to paint as half-aware of its own identity as a force in politics, conscious, that is, that it was pleasant to take part in deme or state affairs as a body and that it was unpleasant to be overridden or abused by aristocrats, not far from realising or at least from acting as if it realised that it could take a very much greater part but still very far indeed from formulating or understanding any formulation of anything like a democratic theory of government – the words that were used to describe the Kleisthenic set-up were still *isonomia* and *isegoria*, equality before the law and, very roughly (it is hard to get the precise sense) equality in the assembly. Both words had much more content in 508 than they would have had in Solon's day but no matter how much more they had, they still fall far short of the positive assertion of *demokratia*.

Kleisthenes certainly shared the popular lack of theory; he had neither the vocabulary nor working models elsewhere in Greece to help him to create a picture of a properly class-conscious and active *demos*. He could observe the men he saw around him and that was all, observe them and the attitude that their growing desire for independence produced; as an aristocrat himself he could not share that desire. He would see, then, that things had changed –

that was all too obvious – but he might well fail to grasp how fundamental the change had been and was to be. A man does not shake
off centuries of aristocratic prejudice overnight and I find it quite
easy to imagine that Kleisthenes, while sensing the general character
of popular discontent and realising that it could now be exploited
by a general appeal to the people as a whole, rather than as a collection of faction followers, could still go on thinking himself in
faction terms, could dream of a new-style following, a new-style
pyramid including the whole *demos*, with Kleisthenes alone per-
ched safely on the top. As a good Athenian Kleisthenes wanted to
give Athens a new and more efficient administration (details of this
important aspect of his work do not concern us); as a good aristocrat he wanted his followers to be happy and was prepared, within
limits, to give them what they wanted; as a shrewd politician he did
his best to design the administration and make his concessions in
such a way that his opponents and only his opponents would suffer;
all that he asked for in return was that his own supporters and the
former supporters of his opponents, together the Athenian *demos*,
should give him the kind of loyalty which he and all aristocrats had
taken for granted in their private following. Given only that,
ostracism would serve its useful function – but would not be turned
on him; the deme organisation would satisfy the *demos*' ambition
but would never cause trouble in an Alkmeonid deme. The only
flaw was that he was expecting a kind of loyalty which in the
nature of things a *demos* cannot give. There is a story in one dis-
reputable source that Kleisthenes himself was ostracised. It is pretty
certainly false. A pity – it would be nice to think that he was hoist
with his own potsherd, and very interesting to know how many men
from his own deme would have voted against him. In other words,
he was relying on the survival of an aristocratic mode of thought
inside a democratic constitution, and, of course, there are societies
in which such things have happened (*mutatis mutandis* Sparta is an
example) but Athens was changing far too fast, Athenians themselves were far too adventurous to allow any such stagnation there.

9 From Kleisthenes to Ephialtes, 508–462 BC

Foreign policy

Kleisthenes, then, set the *demos* free, confident that an Alkmeonid tail would continue to wag the unchained dog. Less than ten years later the dog wagged its tail in complete rejection of the policy on which Kleisthenes and his Alkmeonid successors had based their plans for Athens' survival. In the event, after twenty years of crisis, the Alkmeonids were proved wrong; Athens not only survived but triumphed and the *demos* took charge of its tail for good.

The issue was one of foreign policy. What should Athens' attitude be to the Persian Empire which by about 540 BC had taken over Asia Minor from the Lydians and, with it, the Greek cities of the eastern Aegean coast? Threatened by further Spartan intervention on behalf of the aristocrats, Kleisthenes had sought an alliance with the Persians. Persia's terms were rejected (and it may be that this was already a sign that Athenian 'loyalty' was less than Kleisthenes expected) but Alkmeonids continued to favour collaboration. This was ruled out, gradually as the immediate argument for it (safety from Sparta) grew less pressing and, more dramatically, when Athens decided to help a rising of the Asiatic Greeks against the Persians in 499. There was much indecision in following up the first bold gesture which sent twenty ships across the Aegean and the ships were withdrawn long before the revolt was crushed in 494. But Athens had in effect invited a Persian invasion of Greece and when that invasion came, first against Athens in 490, then against the whole of Greece in 480–479, she was committed to resistance or complete submission. On any rational grounds resistance was absurd yet, extraordinarily, Athenian hoplites drove a Persian army into the sea at Marathon in 490, killing over 6,000 for the loss of 192, and at Salamis in 480 a predominantly Athenian Greek navy, under Spartan command but acting on an Athenian-inspired strategy, broke the vastly larger Persian fleet and sent what was left of it scurrying back across the Aegean.

The enormous Persian army and fleet (there were certainly not less than 600 ships and perhaps a quarter of a million men) had

The burial mound (*Soros*) of the 192 Athenians who
fell at Marathon. It stands at or near the centre of the
battlefield and the view from it (page 152) shows
the plain over which the Athenian hoplites advanced
'at the double' from their camp in the hills
to face the vastly greater Persian force.

overrun the whole of Greece north of the isthmus of Korinth and
even when, after Salamis, the Persian King, Xerxes, and the bulk of
the army retreated to Asia Minor, a force was left behind that
should have been large enough to deal with the combined Greek
army. It took another great battle on land, at Plataia in 479, to
free the mainland, and yet another, tradition said on the same day,
at Mykale in Asia Minor, to destroy the remainder of the fleet and to
ensure the safety of the islands and of the Asiatic Greeks. In these

Gravestone of Aristion, by the sculptor Aristokles, *c.* 500 BC. On *stelai* of this type young men were regularly shown as athletes, older men as soldiers.

Athens played a smaller part; the whole campaign was a united Greek victory but, as Herodotos says (vii, 139), 'A man who called the Athenians the saviours of Greece would not fall short of the truth.' Their homes and their temples had been destroyed, their fields laid waste (in 480 and again in 479 when the Persians had occupied the whole of Attika the Athenians had fled *en masse* to the Peloponnese and to the island of Salamis) but they gained far more than they lost, in prestige and, above all, in self-confidence. It is no surprise that when Sparta refused to stay at the head of an offensive war on Persia Athens hesitated not a moment to form a new association of islanders and Asiatic Greeks 'to take revenge for what they had suffered by ravaging the King's land', a free association to which all contributed ships, men, or money and where all had a say in the policy-making synods which met at Delos, but from the start with Athenian generals and Athenian treasurers. It was not very long before, with allied laziness and Athenian energy, it became in effect an Athenian Empire.

It is against this background that we must interpret the political development of the half century after Kleisthenes. At first sight the evidence does not seem helpful. In 487 BC, we are told, sortition was introduced (or reintroduced: see p. 164) in place of direct election for the archonship which had been used since 510, in the event a change of some significance for it meant that very soon the tribal generals, the *strategoi*, annually elected but eligible for repeated election, took over the archons' role as the leading political figures, thus preparing the way for the prolonged supremacy of a Perikles. But of the men behind the change, of their motives at the time or of their arguments nothing is known.

Beyond this there is no trace of any serious domestic issue dividing Athenians until we reach the moment of the constitutional changes of 462 which established the final form of Athenian democracy. Between 479 and 462, as before 479, political debate at Athens was focused, it would appear, on foreign policy. Superficially it was still the same debate, whether or not to fight Persia, but in a very different context and with very different emphasis.

No one, of course, is likely to have opposed the formation of an offensive anti-Persian League in the Aegean, but it was possible to argue, even in 478, and became increasingly reasonable to argue as the Persian danger receded, that there was another enemy nearer home who resented Athens' new-found distinction and was ready to undermine it even at the risk of war – Sparta – and consequently to suggest that a mere succession of punitive expeditions towards the east, however successful, however profitable, however glorious, was not enough; that a lot of diplomacy and perhaps a little military effort in the Peloponnese, even at the cost of slackening off against Persia, would bring the far more substantial reward of seeing Athens' only rival for supremacy in Greece so entangled with hostile neighbours that she would have to accept the rivalry or even leadership of Athens without a serious struggle.

The man who proposed these arguments and, so far as he was able, tried to act on them throughout the 'seventies was Themistokles, who had himself in 483 persuaded the Athenians to build the ships with which Persia had been defeated and had devised the strategy which won the decisive victory at Salamis. But with characteristic insight and energy, though with a certain lack of immediate political sense, he had turned his thoughts from Persia to Sparta as soon as the final victory was gained and left to others the reward of easy popularity which could be won in the Aegean by collecting the profits of his own earlier foresight (immediately after the Persian retreat he outwitted a Spartan attempt to prevent the rebuilding of Athens' walls by keeping them busy in negotiations while every able Athenian was being employed to throw together some sort of defensible circuit). This change of direction was for him a fatal error; by 470 he had been ostracised and not long afterwards slanderous accusations of intrigue with Persia against Greece, accusations, of course, to which his own current policy lent some plausibility, brought at a time when the League had just won the most glorious success of its career at the Battle of Eurymedon (469), led to condemnation for treachery and flight to the court of the Persian King.

But Themistoklean policy did not die with Themistokles' own disgrace. In 460 Athens found herself at war with Sparta (the so-called First Peloponnesian War of 460–445), and, although the direct evidence for linking the men who led her towards this war with Themistokles is thin, the link can hardly be doubted. They were the same men, the young Perikles and his leader, the shadowy but impressive Ephialtes, who, two years before, had introduced and carried the measures which removed the last traces of aristocratic privilege from the Athenian constitution.

It is, then, certain that in the domestic debate of 462 Athenians were broadly speaking divided into the same two camps which had fought the foreign policy issue in the years before. Then, at least, the Persia/Sparta quarrel could not be separated from, even if it was not derived from, what we can now almost call ideological differences (for one thing Sparta may well have already attracted something of that worship as a paragon of political backwardness which was to become so marked and so corrupting later in the century). But, even if the sources give no more than an occasional hint to help, I am sure that this same connection can be traced back through the preceding years, that to be anti-Spartan in 479 was to be a 'radical', whatever the word might mean in the context, just as it was in 462, and that we can with the help of this assumption reconstruct the 'parties' of the period in home affairs and even guess at their differences with some confidence. This, in large part, because the domestic quarrel of 462 itself looked back as well as, indeed rather than, forwards.

The Areopagos

To explain. Kleisthenes had done little to alter the central government of Athens; in particular he had done nothing to lessen the competence of the old aristocratic council, the Areopagos. The details of its powers are unknown but at least it had some kind of control over the magistrates (it probably heard charges against them when they left office), some sort of general supervision over the body of the law (probably to the extent of seeing that it was internally consistent); wide direct judicial powers, either as a court in its own right, or as an advisory body for the archons in their own courts; for all we know it may also have had many of the powers which in the later fifth century were performed by the Council of 500. It is only assumption that Kleisthenes gave his Council more than its predecessor had had. But far more important than any specific powers must have been the simple undefined and undefinable authority which any such aristocratic body has, the authority of the institution itself and the combined authority of its members at any given moment, all of them ex-magistrates and many of them leading political figures of the day. Powers can easily be removed by legislation and the removal of its powers was the core of the reforms of 462 – thereafter the Areopagos retained the right to try cases of homicide and a few other crimes which were thought to have religious significance; everything else was transferred to the Council of 500, the Assembly or the popular courts which Solon had established to hear appeals; the remarkable thing is that with its powers the Areopagos seems to have lost much of its authority as well; this at once and almost without a struggle. The only possible explanation is that the authority was already weaker than the powers which gave expression to it, that the Areopagos was already regarded by the mass of Athenians, consciously or unconsciously, as an anomaly in the constitution of 462, that is in the constitution of 508.

In 508 it had not been so regarded, either by Kleisthenes, or, it would seem, by those who had followed him. How does such a change come about? The introduction of sortitive election must have helped. Between 510 and 487 the archons had been the elected leaders of Athens. With more than twenty years of such recruits among its numbers the Areopagos must have been an able and impressive body. But after 487 although the men who held the archonship and passed into the Areopagos still belonged to the top two census classes, they were little more than a random cross-section of the aristocracy, not aristocrats who had been chosen by the

An Attic red-figure plate of about 520–510 BC by the Cerberus painter. Outside the figure of a mounted archer in Scythian dress runs the faint inscription 'Miltiades is fair'. This may well be the Miltiades who was sent out by Hippias to be tyrant of the Athenian settlement on the Chersonese (Hellespontine), was ejected from there by the Persians in 493 and returned to direct the Athenian victory at Marathon.

people; by 462 the Areopagos must have lost much of its real character as a forum for the country's political élite. But this is not enough – a body like the Areopagos does not fail just because it is stupid or unrepresentative. The change to sortition, indeed, is more likely to be a symptom of a shift of attitude than a cause of it, and it is the shift of attitude that matters.

Somehow or other what was natural in 508 was absurd in 462; absurd in fact because, with the slightest push the Areopagos disappeared as a political force for the rest of the century. To support it was simply foolish.

Conservative arguments

But many Athenians still did, while the aristocrats themselves were sufficiently shocked by its fate to assassinate Ephialtes soon after his success and to think of betraying Athens to Sparta during the war which followed.

If, then, we are to get any clue to the history of the preceding years, we must first try to understand how both sides felt when the choice was given them by Ephialtes and Perikles on the day when a majority accepted what we now call 'full democracy'.

The leading supporter of the Areopagos was a certain Kimon, aristocrat by birth (he was the son of Miltiades, hero of the Battle of Marathon) and in his marriage (he had married an Alkmeonid girl). But, aristocrat as he was, he it was who had profited from Themistokles' abdication in 479, who had commanded the forces of the Delian League in all its most important campaigns thereafter and, until 465, with brilliant success; inevitably some of the glamour that surrounded the young hero must have reflected on his policy, glamorous enough in itself, of pursuing the war against Persia and of collaborating with Sparta, some of it too on his friends, other aristocrats, and on the institution which embodied their ideal, the Areopagos. Hence one argument: an aristocracy produces men like Kimon and a noble policy – do not change a winning and sentimentally attractive team.

The only other argument I can see is at first sight equally irrational, the natural conservative argument that any change is dangerous, more specifically that some element of fear is necessary to keep ordinary men in order, that courts composed of other ordinary men could never acquire the majesty or the authority of an Areopagos. At first sight irrational, but only because we know that in the event it was proved to be so. At the time it could have been a serious doubt which the radicals somehow had to answer.

Radical answers

At the level of street-corner politics their answers to both arguments were easy ones. In 465 Kimon had suffered his first serious defeat when attempting to found a new Athenian colony in Thrace; for the next two years he was occupied in the ultimately successful but wholly unglamorous and difficult siege of Thasos, a revolted ally not a barbarian enemy. When he returned in 463 he was prosecuted (it is true, acquitted) for corruption; so were other individual Areopagites. So the hero's halo was set awry, the image of his venerable associates a little tarnished. He was still able to persuade the Athenians to send an army to help the Spartans against the menace of a helot revolt in 462 but, almost at once, Spartan suspicion sent him and his army home in disgrace; his pre-eminence, already challenged in 463, was broken.

So the argument from success disintegrated; the argument from conservatism needed more ingenuity to counter, but it was done quite neatly by the claim that the radicals themselves were the real conservatives, that there had been a time (we do not know if one was specified) when the Areopagos had lacked its present powers and these it had usurped over the years. The claim, of course, was true in the sense that before Solon no one would or could have said 'The Areopagos has such and such a power' – definition was at the earliest Solon's work – but it was completely false in fact. The Areopagos' activity would become more noticeable and therefore more easily resented as Athenians grew up politically but it is hard to believe that Areopagites had ever been less influential in fact than they were in 462. The claim is also interesting in that it is the earliest clear example we have of a theoretical approach to politics – usurpation is a charge that can be made only in a society which believes that its constitution is sanctioned by something other than its mere existence – and indeed there is an air of the doctrinaire about this whole revolution which is quite lacking in earlier crises (Solon had worked on what were moral rather than constitutional principles). But whatever its truth or interest this is a debating-point, not a serious case. For that we have to turn to the theatre.

Aeschylos, for me the greatest of the three Athenian tragedians, was a radical and in 457 BC he produced what I believe to be the radicals' justification of their reforms, the trilogy known as the *Oresteia*. Agamemnon, setting out for Troy, was ordered by the gods to sacrifice his daughter; by all the traditional rules of vengeance his wife, Klytemnestra, must take blood for blood and on his return from Troy Agamemnon in his turn was murdered; but by those same rules his son, Orestes, was bound to kill his own mother and Klytemnestra died; the role of avenger now fell to the Furies and, in the name of justice, Orestes was hounded through Greece by these hideous creatures, though he had done no more than his duty, itself impressed upon him by the gods. Thus far the debate is outside time and space, but in his flight Orestes comes to Athens and suddenly the place is an Athenian court, the time, a curious compound of past and present, with the present well to the fore. The court too is a mixture. Athena herself founds it specially to hear this case of homicide and calls it the Areopagos, yet in presiding over its first case she follows the procedure of a magistrate in those popular courts to which Perikles and Ephialtes had given much of the Areopagos' business. And finally, when this blend of old and new acquitted Orestes, the Furies too were found a permanent home in Athens, beneath the rock where the Areopagos met, but only a hundred yards or so from the Heliaia, and, with their new home acquired a new name, the Eumenides, the 'kindly ones'.

With all these different levels in play, abstract justice and practical justice, ancient Athens and modern Athens, it is not easy to be certain about Aeschylos' attitude, particularly when we know so little about the precise political context in which the trilogy was produced. But there is one safe starting point. A man who represented the foundation of the Areopagos as the foundation of a homicide court accepted the radical argument on usurpation, welcomed the changes of 462. But why, in that case, is the Areopagos so praised, why, in particular, are the Furies, the embodiment of primitive, i.e. aristocratic justice, welcomed to the new society, why does Athena say, at one point, 'we must not drive *to deinon*, the awe-inspiring, the terrible, out of our city'? (*v.* 698) Is Aeschylos perhaps a 'moderate'? I do not think so. We need only assume that the reformers of 462 were serious, thinking men, not irresponsible revolutionaries, or at least that they could be supported by thinking men, for everything to fall into place. This, in fact, is the real answer to the conservative argument. 'You say that men will lose their respect for the law if its administration is taken out of hands which are awe-inspiring in their own right. You are wrong. Respect for the law is bad if it is only fear of the horrible; it can be transformed into something better. The popular courts and the Areopagos are both courts, and courts serve the law; it is the law itself that men should respect, not any privileged body which administers it. The new Athenian legal system, Areopagos, Heliaia and the Furies all rolled into one, can work.' It did.

The real issue

Neither Aeschylos nor his political allies need have nor would have formulated their case in these terms, nor need they have been fully conscious of its implication – that in attacking the Areopagos they were merely applying more rigorously a principle which had been introduced by Solon and, even if accidentally, accepted by Kleisthenes, that the constitution or the law should be independent of and more important than any man or group of men who administered them, or, to put it the other way round and in more Kleisthenic terms, that no kind of personal authority, whether backed by religious or aristocratic tradition (always closely intertwined) or by any other kind of pressure, should be allowed to operate except in so far as it was sanctioned by the constitution or the law. But whatever terms they used, however unaware they may have been of their programme's place in the history of constitutional principle, they were in fact appealing to the past in making their proposals, they were merely asserting in one area of government what had already been asserted in others, they had had more than a generation of practice in applying the idea of constitutional life, and more than a generation in which to find the idea of personal authority both strange and irksome. In the Areopagos alone some of this authority still remained and it was therefore an anomaly, an anomaly best removed by destroying such constitutional sanction as it still had on which to rest its para-constitutional influence.

This point is vital. Modern historians have sometimes explained the changes of 462 as the result of the appearance of a new class in politics, the men of the newly established and now triumphant fleet, the *thetes*; they have gone on to see the changes as a great leap forward in the dark into a new type of constitution – the so-called 'radical democracy'. If I am right both of these views are unlikely to be true. No doubt many *thetes* were now in a position to take part in politics, no doubt their arrival modified the look of the assembly and the courts, but, as we have seen (pp. 21–8), there is no good reason to see them as a class apart from the rest of the Athenian *demos*. As they began to play a part, they joined and, of course, strengthened those who were already active, they did not stand against them, nor, on my interpretation of 462, is there any reason to think that the rest of the *demos* was not itself beginning to accept wholeheartedly, even to some extent consciously, the Solonian and Kleisthenic principle, was not beginning to see the Areopagos as an absurd hangover from an earlier age. Every Athenian, whatever his class, gained in political power; only Areopagites stood to lose, and, so long as we make some allowance (not very much) for the greater natural conservatism of the well-to-do, I cannot believe, Areopagites apart, that there was any noticeable division among Athenians on class lines on this issue.

But more important than that, the hoplites and *thetes* who voted for Ephialtes were not thinking in terms of a great leap forward in the dark. No one would deny that 462 *was* a turning point in

Athenian history; after the rebuff to Kimon, Athens broke with Sparta and, whether at war or not, remained hostile until the final outbreak in 431; after the Areopagos lost its powers (and with the introduction of pay for jury service which came at about the same time), the democratic courts became and remained one of the most striking features of Athenian life; but the men responsible would see the changes as a tidying-up of the Kleisthenic system, not as the creation of a hitherto unimagined Utopia. In foreign policy they were accepting what Themistokles had preached since 479, in home affairs they were merely giving constitutional form to the results of a process begun in 508 or even before and continued at varying pace through the intervening years.

This being so it is fairly easy to measure how far the ordinary Athenian had moved in these fifty years. In 508 he was discontented with the factional squabbling of the aristocracy; this Kleisthenes had sensed. But he was still subservient enough for Kleisthenes to mistake the general discontent for a specific grudge against his own, Kleisthenes', enemies – how else could he have thought that he would retain his own position? In all probability the ordinary man himself still thought more in terms of specific grudges than general principles; he would assert his independence if provoked, he would not assume responsibility as a matter of course. And here is the essence of the change – by 462 the ordinary Athenian, let me add again hoplites as well as *thetes*, came to assume responsibility as a matter of course.

The clearest illustration of this is in the sphere of law – in 508 the Heliaia was still a court of appeal, it existed merely to prevent injustices; in 462 it became a court of first instance, it took over control of justice. And even this, striking as it appears at first sight, may have been in fact far less of an innovation than it seems. In 594 the archon gave a verdict in his court and the dissatisfied litigant could appeal; after 462 the archon still held a preliminary hearing to decide if there was a case and then referred the case for trial to an appropriate popular court. As an assertion of the *demos'* legal authority the official imposition of this procedure is indeed important but it need not have made any great change in practice, given only that by 462 appeal had gradually become a regular thing; something very like the later system could easily have been created *de facto* by the archons' realisation that in the face of almost certain appeal it was hardly worth his while to take the first 'trial' seriously. We do not know to what extent if at all this was the case, but here again it is at least possible that a slow change of emphasis in the years before was just as important as the actual legislation which gave it recognition.

The same change of emphasis runs all through: in 508 the *demos* elected its aristocratic leaders and on all important matters decided on the policy they were to follow (though as late as 489 the hero of Marathon, Miltiades, could ask the *demos* for a fleet without telling it the object of his expedition) but I suspect that once elected the leader was very much a leader; in 462 aristocrats were still chosen for high office but they were chosen as servants of the *demos*. Things have moved a long way since Solon could put forward as the purpose – and at the time a progressive purpose – of his legislation that 'thus the *demos* will best follow its leaders'.

The principle is proclaimed in another Aeschylean play, the *Suppliants*, probably of 463, where a mythical king answers a plea for protection with very unkinglike thoughts: 'You are not suppliants at *my* door. It is the whole city which risks pollution and the whole city must find the answer.' 'But you are the city,' the suppliants reply and press his personal responsibility. He answers: 'I have said it before. Whatever my power, I may not do this without the demos.' (*vv.* 365–401)

And here at last is the domestic issue – not an issue of public debate but simply of public behaviour – on which the politicians of the period divide; there were some who would help to change the emphasis, others who would not. The Alkmeonids, shocked by popular disloyalty after 508, looked around for new friends; at first they tried the exiled tyrant Hippias, now at the Persian court; but when their policy of appeasement failed so miserably at Marathon, they allied themselves with Kimon, and, we may suppose, others of like mind, and they cemented their alliance in the traditional way – by marriage. These men, the bulk of the Athenian aristocracy, accepted democracy, but they accepted it only because they had to – they continued to think and, so far as it was possible, to behave like aristocrats.

There is a revealing tale that Kimon won great popularity by his generosity towards members of his deme: 'Any one of them could come to him every day and receive enough to support him. Besides his whole estate was unfenced so that anyone could help himself to the produce.' (Aristotle, *Athenian Constitution*, 27). In other words he was still the open-handed local dynast at heart. The same story goes on to say that Perikles outbid him for popular support by introducing jurors' pay – not for him personal largesse among his private retinue, he was a class politician – and whether the story is true or false it sums up perfectly the difference between the two men. The introduction about 464 of state-burial for those who fell in battle is another example of the same kind of thinking. The state should take over from the family responsibility for those who have died in its service.

But it was not only Perikles and his associates in the 'sixties who played by these new rules. Inside the Alkmeonid faction of 508 there were already some younger men who not only understood but welcomed the change that Kleisthenes brought – Aristeides, nick-named 'the Just', founder of the Delian League, and Xanthippos, father of Perikles, later to be joined by Themistokles.

It is easy to go too far, to take Themistokles' interest in the navy, for example, as a sign that he was deliberately encouraging the growth of that thetic class which has been seen as the active force behind 'radical democracy' but there are limits to the foresight even of a genius and the threat from Persia is an adequate enough motive for a naval programme. But that Themistokles and his friends accepted wholeheartedly and gladly the results of Kleisthenes' constitution there can be no doubt. They had no programme of further democratic reform that we know of – there was no need for one as yet – but all three are described in the sources as friends and champions of the *demos*. This can only mean that they saw and to some extent understood the changes going on around them; moreover that they were ready to encourage them.

The weapon of ostracism was left unused for some twenty years after Kleisthenes had devised it; then suddenly between 487 and 482 five leading politicians were packed off to a ten-year exile by the *demos*' votes. The explanation is twofold. On the one hand the *demos* had at last acquired the confidence to use its strength (the victory at Marathon would have played its part), on the other there were politicians around who were prepared to let it use it, even to urge it to use it. Most historians have agreed in seeing, and surely rightly, the influence of Themistokles behind this series of decisions, and, whatever his immediate motives may have been in the individual cases, the method that he chose to use, a method that gave full responsibility to the *demos*, is revealing – he was a conscious democrat.

It is this consciousness, this awareness of the new society and of what could be made of it that give the reforms of 462 that touch of the doctrinaire which I have already mentioned. It is the same consciousness which produces, at some time in the second quarter of the century, a new word to describe the new ideal. For the late sixth century *isegoria* and *isonomia* were enough; now the emphasis was shifted to *demokratia*.

10 The great debate

Democratic conservatism

The Athenian *demokratia* was founded on two cardinal principles: an absolute acceptance of the laws (including what we would call the constitution), of what I have not very elegantly called a depersonalised administration, and on the belief that everyone who was admitted to the society governed by these laws had an equal right and almost an equal duty to administer and maintain them. Credit for the first must go largely to Solon, although he did not begin the movement towards it nor did he succeed as well as he hoped in establishing it. Credit for the second can be shared among a number of leading politicians, Solon, Peisistratos, Kleisthenes (if only by accident), Ephialtes and Perikles, but the largest share does not belong to any politician; it must be given to the Athenians as a whole, to those of them who agitated for the changes and even more to those of them, the majority, who were prepared to accept them and to show at every stage that they were capable of facing the responsibilities they were given.

So too the credit for maintaining these principles, except for two brief periods in 411 and in 404, throughout the next century and more. And the emphasis must be on the word 'maintaining' – the average Athenian after 462 was a conservative, anxious to preserve what he had, not to initiate anything new; this for the simple reason that in all important ways what he had was what he wanted.

This is not to say that the complexion of Athenian politics remained constant. Indeed on the surface there was another drastic development in 429 when Perikles died and, Aristotle says (*Athenian Constitution*, 28), 'for the first time the people chose a leader who was not respected by the upper-class' i.e. was not a member of one of the traditional ruling families. This was Kleon, a wealthy manufacturer and son of a wealthy manufacturer, the first outstanding example of a long line of similar men, the so-called 'demagogues', rich, able, sometimes brilliant, but scarcely 'gentlemen' – at least not in the eyes of gentlemen. The explanation of their rise is simple; the economic development of Athens was gradually

Tokens probably used for allotment to office.
The upper half carries the name of a deme
(here Halimous), the bottom perhaps an abbreviation
of the office. On the reverse the name of a tribe ran
across both halves. The precise mechanics
of their use is not known.

but steadily putting more and more emphasis on manufacture, rather than or at least as well as on land, as a source of wealth; at the same time it was making increased demands on politicians, for the administration of a large and complex state needs professional skill not simply aristocratic flair. These men were just as able, perhaps more able to acquire this skill than the aristocrat, and as the Assembly, with growing confidence, took more and more state business into its own hands, away from the executive, it was easy to use their talents, provided only that they were competent orators, to direct policy without holding any office, such as the *strategia*, which required techniques (military for example) which they did not have and did not claim. It is no surprise that in the end their skill was rewarded, even if they did lack that magical quality of 'leadership' which aristocrats still liked to think was theirs alone.

But, for all the stir that it caused at the time, the appearance of the demagogues is not really a sign of sudden change. In theory the Ephialtic constitution permitted, even encouraged them, while in practice they had been moving up in the world of politics for at least a generation before their final success. Even Themistokles had been, comparatively, an outsider ('an upstart' Herodotos calls him (vii, 143), a second-class aristocrat whose family still lived outside Athens (near Sounion) at the end of the sixth century; more significantly, towards the middle of the century there is some evidence to suggest that several other lesser aristocrats and even more hitherto completely obscure families were edging their way into the lower levels of the administration.

Fragment of an inscription recording payments
made by the treasurers in the year 415–414 BC,
one for the celebration of a festival, others for
the troops in Melos and for the Sicilian
campaign; one part of Athens' increasingly
complex financial administration.

In other words the demagogues are no more than the natural result of Athens' growth and of Kleisthenes' assault on aristocratic power and, when they finally emerge, they are as conservative in their outlook as any other Athenian. Such agitation as there was for change came from a very different quarter, from the right, and it was agitation for a return to something like aristocracy, or, as we must call it in its new artificial and theoretical form, oligarchy.

Oligarchic reaction

Three factors combined to produce it. First that the generation which was entering politics in the 420s did not remember the crisis of 462; for them full democracy was something to be taken for granted, something that they could no longer get excited about, for or against. Secondly, that the upper-class of this generation was the first that had had to face the claims of men like Kleon to complete recognition; the supremacy of the aristocrat Perikles had softened the blow which they should have felt and for a short time did feel in 462 – they had murdered Ephialtes soon after his success. Now they came face to face with the real implications of democracy. Thirdly, that this same generation was the first to feel the full effects of a new intellectual revolution, the growth of a class of professional scholars and teachers, the so-called sophists, who began to apply the principles of Ionian science to fields more relevant to political life, to rhetoric, political theory, philosophy in our sense, and the like. Trained by these men, the young aristocrat of the 420s could stand apart from society and turn his ordinary human prejudice against a man like Kleon into a critique of democracy as such.

One such young man was the so-called 'Old Oligarch' (above, p. 102). The modern name should not mislead – there is nothing old about this excited, immature undergraduate essayist. He has been given new toys of style and thought, is playing with both and is none too competent with either. Nor is there any doubt about the source of the toys: little tricks of language, the structure of the argument point straight to the sophists; so, above all, does the principle

A late copy of
a bust of Perikles,
one of several which
are probably based on a
work in bronze by Perikles'
contemporary, Kresilas.

on which he builds his whole case – 'Every man has the right to look after his own interests'. It is no great step from there to 'Justice is the interest of the stronger', the claim of another contemporary sophist, Thrasymachos, a claim which Plato wrote the *Republic* to refute.

And given this principle he erects a case which in fact makes nonsense of the second part of his name as well. Democracy he grants is inefficient and corrupt; its leaders, the demagogues, are stupid, common profiteers. But the *demos* is strong, unshakeably strong, and knows that the leadership of the demagogues, with all the attendant waste and foolishness, in fact is in its interests – and 'every man has a right to look after his own interests'. It is just conceivable, I suppose, that a practising oligarch could write like this, but if he did he was an oligarch in absolute despair. Far more probably he is not an oligarch at all. He is a young man who is just learning to analyse his society, who doesn't much like the results of his analysis, but who will, when the time comes to enter political life, accept society as it is, however distasteful, and make the best of it – on his own admission there was no alternative.

And when he enters politics how will he behave? Another young man of similar background points towards the answer. Aristophanes in his *Knights*, produced in 424 when the comedian was about twenty years old, starts from almost exactly the same premises. *Demos* himself is put on the stage, a greedy and, apparently, muddle-headed old man, deaf to the advice of his honest slaves, wholly bewitched by one crooked slave (Kleon) whose only thought is to line his own pockets while keeping his master happy with flattery. But, as it turns out, Demos is not the fool he seems:

> CHORUS: Proud, O Demos, thy sway.
> Thee, as tyrant and king,
> All men fear and obey.
> Yet, O yet, 'tis a thing
> Easy to lead thee astray.
> Empty fawning and praise
> Pleased thou art to receive;

All each orator says
Sure at once to believe;
Wit thou hast, but 'tis roaming;
Ne'er we find it its home in.

DEMOS: Wit there's none in your hair.
What, you think me a fool!
What, you know not I wear,
Wear my motley by rule!
Well all day do I fare,
Nursed and cockered by all;
Pleased to fatten and train
One prime thief in my stall.
When, full gorged with his gain,
Up that instant I snatch him,
Strike one blow and despatch him.

CHORUS: Art thou really so deep?
Is such artfulness thine?
Well for all if thou keep
Firm to this thy design.
Well for all if, as sheep
Marked for victims, thou feed
These thy knaves in the Pnyx,
Then, if dainties thou need,
Haste on a victim to fix;
Slay the fattest and finest;
There's thy meal when thou dinest.

DEMOS: Ah! They know not that I
Watch them plunder and thieve,
Ah! 'tis easy, they cry,
Him to gull and deceive.
Comes *my* turn by and by!
Down their gullet, full quick,
Lo, my verdict-tube coils,
Turns them giddy and sick,
Up they vomit their spoils.
Such with rogues is my dealing,
'tis for *myself* they are stealing.

(*Knights*, 1111–1150, tr. B. B. Rogers)

Just as the Old Oligarch said – with despair. But in comedy there can be a happy ending. Kleon the vulgar tanner can be supplanted in Demos' heart by an even more vulgar sausage-seller who will out-shout, outbid and outflatter. So indeed he does – and just to make the ending even happier – the sausage-seller turns out to have a heart of gold. The heart of gold is comic fantasy but the moral of the sausage-seller's success could easily be applied outside the theatre. The young aristocrat with political ambitions must not imitate a Perikles, still less a Kimon, he must put on the demagogue's clothes and beat a Kleon at his own game, he must become a sausage-seller. And that, after all, was no great problem for a clever young man who knew that he had been equipped with all the newest tricks of the trade by the best teachers in Greece.

The tragedy of it was that they were setting out to imitate not Kleon but their own idea of Kleon. We all admit in some degree that the end can justify the means, that a politician cannot be blamed too much if he plays the political game according to the rules of his day, but there must be a worthwhile end. We can see in Kleon's career a consistent policy designed for the welfare of Athens and her allies and for the preservation of democracy; they saw only an unscrupulous and vulgar campaign for personal profit and power and it was this that they tried to imitate.

Many must have tried and failed – tutored mediocrity, whatever they may have believed, is no real substitute for untutored genius. A course in politics will not make a Perikles any more than a course in business will make a magnate or a diploma in education a Sokrates. But some of them had a touch of genius too, one more than most – Alkibiades, whose brilliant, erratic and irresponsible career is woven into the whole story of Athens' failure. Brought up in Perikles' household he seems to have acquired little from his background but the assumption of a right to inherit Perikles' position and in the negotiations which led to the Peace of Nikias (421), a temporary break in the Peloponnesian War, and in the uneasy years that followed, he appears at the heart of a series of tricks and schemes (Melos and Syrakuse are two of them) which would have made even the sausage-seller blush. He was the perfect 'demagogue'. But in the early months of the Sicilian expedition where he shared the command, he was recalled to Athens and rather than face trouble at home fled to Sparta. There he told the truth, about himself and about others who were still playing the democratic game in Athens:

Our city had a democracy and we simply had to accept it, although we did try to moderate the excesses to which others tried to lead the mob. And so we retained control, although everyone with any sense recognised democracy for what it was. But there is no point in trying to say anything new about an acknowledged folly. Only remember that it was too dangerous to try to change it in the middle of a war. (paraphrase of Thucydides, vi, 89)

In 415 the 'acknowledged folly' was still as unshakeable as it had been ten years before when the 'Old Oligarch' wrote. But in Sicily in 413 Athens lost her navy and her wealth, the navy which he had seen as the guarantee of democracy and the wealth which gave the *demos* its only motive for democracy. By all the rules, his rules, oligarchy was now a practical possibility, and the sausage-sellers of 415 became the oligarchs of 411. The miserable failure of their revolution (above, p. 12) is clear enough proof that his rules were wrong, that self-interest, crude self-interest, was not the only motive that Athenians had for liking democracy, that the fine phrases of a Kleon, or for that matter of a Perikles (below, p. 233–4) about a people's right and duty to rule were not just an empty sham, that ordinary men really did believe that democracy was a good thing.

It could be argued that this is a biased view. So it is, in so far as it suggests that the Athenians' faith in democracy was justifiable. I happen to share that faith, but I may be wrong. But I do not think that there is any bias in this condemnation of the opposition, for at least one of its ablest sympathisers is our best evidence for it. In the early fourth century Plato, who had grown up among the oligarchs of 411 and 404, looked back and judged the generation which had produced them. He was too much an oligarch himself to appreciate the principles of democracy but he did see the weakness

The speaker's rostrum (*bema*) on the Pnyx; the members of the assembly stood in a roughly semicircular area to the left of the photograph. Probably until 508 BC the assembly met in the Agora; after the fourth century in the theatre of Dionysos. For the period between, this was the site but the physical arrangements did not remain constant throughout. Themistokles and Perikles did not actually use this platform but they stood not far away.

of his friends, he realised that politics played without a purpose produces disaster.

In Plato's dialogue, the *Gorgias*, Sokrates discusses with the great sophist Gorgias and his not over-clever pupil, Polos, the value of their favourite subject, rhetoric, and, of course, defeats them both, but gently; Gorgias is old and honest and deserving respect as master of his subject, Polos is young and rude but hardly clever enough to earn rough treatment; both, in any case, are academics and hardly matter. But Sokrates' next opponent is not an academic; Kallikles, a brilliant young pupil of Gorgias who will go out and apply the lessons he has learnt in the real world of politics, and at once the atmosphere of the dialogue changes. Gorgias and Polos exaggerated the power of rhetoric; innocently they believed that it did some good. But Kallikles has no such illusions – rhetoric does indeed do good but it is only good for him. The weak may shelter behind the laws but the strong should despise them and seek the only worthwhile goal, self-interest, a goal which in a democracy rhetoric helps to put within his reach. There is no mistaking Plato's horror at this doctrine. It is worth paraphrasing Sokrates' words:

So do as I say Kallikles and follow me on this path [the study of real justice]. It is the one that leads to happiness. If others despise or insult you, ignore them; you will come to no harm by practising goodness. And then, when we have practised it together, then and then only let us turn to politics, for it would be a crime to do so in our present state. We are so uneducated. Our argument shows that the best way of life lies in the pursuit of justice, so let us follow that path and urge others to do the same, ignoring the one which you recommend. For it is valueless, Kallikles.

Young men like Kallikles or Alkibiades were the innovators in late fifth-century Athens and indeed it was their cleverness, their desire for innovation that destroyed Athenian unity and lost her the Peloponnesian War. Against reverence for the laws they argued (as the sophists had rightly taught them though they drew the wrong conclusion) that law was no more than convention; and, contradictorily, that the laws of Solon (or Kleisthenes or Drakon), versions of which they invented to suit their own tastes, were more worthy of reverence than the current system. Against the system itself they argued that only the educated, the clever should be trusted with political decisions, that democracy was stupid and even unfair in that it gave no extra voice to intelligence and worth.

The democrats' case

In reply Kleon could appeal to sentiment and to tradition, setting himself up as the heir of Themistokles or Perikles, ranging himself with the older generation who had voted for Ephialtes and still had a positive interest in the privileges their votes had won for them. But he could also produce a reasoned argument:

Bad laws that stay unchanged are better than good laws which are unstable; stupidity combined with restraint is better than unbridled cleverness. It is the ordinary man, not the clever one who manages a city well. The latter always wants to seem wiser than the laws . . . but the former mistrusts his own cleverness . . . and acting as judge rather than competitor, arrives more often at the true answer. So we must not let ourselves be carried away by ingenuity or intellectual rivalry into offering ideas to you the people simply for effect. (Thucydides, iii. 37)

A Syrakusan democrat, faced with the same problem a few years later, put the same case more directly:

It may be said that democracy is neither wise nor fair, that men of property are also best fitted to rule. But I say, first that the word *demos* includes the whole state, oligarchy only a part; next that the rich may be the best guardians of property, the wise the best advisers but that none can hear and decide as well as the many; and that all these talents receive their due in a democracy. An oligarchy on the other hand gives the many their share of the dangers but itself takes not just the largest share but the whole of the profit. This is what the powerful among you and the younger generation are aiming at, but in a great city they cannot possibly attain it. (Thucydides, vi, 3)

Neither statement, perhaps, is very moving, but both men are on the defensive; for a full and positive assertion of the democrat's ideal we must turn to the famous speech which Perikles gave at the public burial of those who died in the first year of the Peloponnesian War:

Above the architrave of a Doric temple ran a frieze of alternating triglyphs (projecting slabs with two vertical grooves on the face and a half-groove at each angle) and metopes, slabs which might be plain or might carry a relief sculpture. This is a sculptured metope from the Parthenon (cf. figures on pages 24 and 40) representing a fight between a Centaur and a Lapith.

We enjoy a constitution in which there is no envy of our neighbours' laws; we are an example to others, not imitators, and this constitution, administered for the many not for the few, we call democracy. Our laws give equal justice to every man in his private disputes; merit, not class, determines a man's reputation, nor is any man's way barred by poverty or obscurity, if he has any contribution to make. Freedom is the keynote of our society in public and in private; we are neither resentful nor offensive if a man does what he likes. But private freedom does not lead to public lawlessness. Fear teaches us to obey the government and the laws . . .

Tombstone of the Athenians who fell at
Potidaia in 432 BC (a preliminary to
the Peloponnesian War) carrying three four-line
metrical epigrams. Above, now lost, was a
relief representing the battle. Below there would
probably have been a list of names.

We pursue beauty without extravagance, culture without softness. We use
our wealth, we do not boast about it, and poverty itself is no disgrace, only
the failure to fight against it. Our politicians manage their own affairs as well
as the city's, our ordinary working man is a shrewd judge in public matters;
and we are the only people who call the man who stands aloof from politics
not just unambitious but useless. All of us are fit to judge if not to originate...

As a city we are a model for the rest of Greece, as individuals no other na-
tion, I am sure, can match the easy versatility of the Athenian. . . . It is for
such a city that these men have fought and died; for such a city that every
one of us is willing to do the same. (Thucydides, ii, 37–41)

The real Athens, the real Athenian no doubt fell far short of
Perikles' ideal but, as I argued at the outset, an audience of ordinary
Athenian men (and women) listened to this speech or something
very like it, understood it and accepted the principles on which the
ideal was based. They also came as near, perhaps, as was humanly
possible to putting those principles into action.

At every turn in Perikles' statement of them there are echoes of
the struggles of the previous centuries – 'Fear teaches us to obey
the laws', as Aeschylos, I have suggested, argued that it could;
'Our laws give equal justice to every man' as Solon had intended
when he 'wrote down laws alike for noble and for commoner'. But
there is an echo of a different sort which best sums up how far the

ordinary Athenian had had to come in the centuries before 431. 'All of us are fit to judge . . . each one of us is willing to fight and die' – Odysseus had had other standards:

But when he found any man of the *demos* giving tongue . . . he rated him severely. 'You there,' he said, 'sit still and wait for orders from your betters, you who are no warrior and a weakling, counting for nothing in battle or debate.'

List of dates

This list of dates is not for Greek History in general, only of the more important events mentioned in the text together with a few others that are relevant. Suggested interpretations (and sometimes the dates themselves) are justified in the text.

BC *c.* 800–775   First known Greek expansion to the east – foundation of Al Mina in Syria from Euboia.

c. 750   First known Greek expansion in the west – foundation of Kyme in Italy.

c. 750   Introduction of the alphabet from the east, perhaps via Al Mina. Homer composes (and writes down?) the *Iliad*, later the *Odyssey*, in Ionia.

c. 735   First Greek colony in Sicily – Naxos from Euboia. Followed very shortly by major Korinthian colonies in Kerkyra and at Syrakuse (*c.* 734), then by many more from Euboia, Achaia, etc.

c. 735–710   Lelantine War – Chalkis, Korinth, Samos and allies against Eretria, Megara, Miletos and allies. Sparta (ally of Chalkis) annexes Messenia. First developments in hoplite technique.

c. 725   Beginnings of oriental influence in Greek art.

c. 700   Hesiod writes *Works and Days* in Boiotia.

c. 680   Gyges seizes the throne of Lydia.

? *c.* 675   Sparta acquires constitution – 'Lykourgan' reforms.

669   Sparta defeated by Argos under King Pheidon at Hysiai.

c. 668–660   Sparta crushes Messenian revolt.

c. 660   Archilochos writes earliest surviving personal poetry.

657   Kypselos establishes tyranny at Korinth, expelling or killing ruling aristocrats (the Bakchiads).

c. 650   Tyrannies established at Sikyon, Megara and elsewhere.

c. 630   Attempt at tyranny by Kylon in Athens. First settlements in North Africa, at Kyrene (from Thera) and Naukratis (from Miletos).

625 Periander succeeds Kypselos at Korinth.

c. 620 Drakon's law code at Athens.

c. 610 First Black Sea colonies (Istros, Olbia, etc.) after at least fifty years of sporadic exploration (traditions of earlier settlements – e.g. at Sinope c. 750 – are unconfirmed).

c. 600 Athens at war with Mytilene over Sigeion in Troad.
Scientific speculation begins with Thales in Miletos.

594 Solon's economic and constitutional legislation at Athens.

585 Death of Periander at Korinth.

582 Collapse of tyranny in Korinth.

561 Peisistratos seizes power in Athens – two short periods of rule and two exiles before final success at Battle of Pallene (546).

c. 550 Sparta adopts policy which leads to formation of Peloponnesian League, nucleus of Greek resistance to Persia in 480.

? c. 550 Anaximander of Miletos draws map of the world.

c. 545 Sparta defeats Argos and annexes Thyrea (west coast of Peloponnese).
Persian conquest of Lydia followed by Persian occupation of Ionia.

528 Hippias succeeds Peisistratos at Athens.

c. 514 Persian army crosses Bosporos into Europe – thence northwards across Danube – defeated by Scythians and withdraws.

514 Murder of Hippias' brother Hipparchos by Harmodios and Aristogeiton.

510 Hippias expelled from Athens by Alkmeonids with Spartan aid.

508 Constitutional reforms of Kleisthenes in Athens.

508–506 Defeat of attempted Spartan, Boiotian and Chalkidian intervention in Athenian affairs.

499   Ionia revolts from Persia, led by Aristagoras of Miletos. Athenian contingent sent to assist.

497   Withdrawal of Athenian forces from Ionia.

494   Defeat of Ionians by Persians at Lade. Fall of Miletos to Persia. Collapse of revolt.

c. 494   Defeat of Argos by Sparta at Sepeia.

490   First Persian invasion of Greece, routed by Athenians at Marathon.

487   First use of ostracism at Athens.

482–480   Building of large Athenian fleet under Themistokles' guidance.

481   Formation of Greek League to resist further Persian invasion, under Spartan leadership.

480   Second Persian invasion under King Xerxes – unsuccessful defence of Thermopylai by allied force under the Spartan King Leonidas – inconclusive sea engagements at Artemision – sack of Attika by Persians – decisive victory by combined Greek fleet at Salamis – withdrawal of Xerxes, leaving Mardonios in command in Greece.

479   Defeat of Mardonios by combined Greek army at Plataia, and of Persians in Asia Minor by Greek fleet at Mykale.

478   Withdrawal of Sparta and Peloponnesian League from Greek fleet. Formation of Athenian-led Delian League to follow up successes.

471   Attempted secession of Naxos from League crushed by force.

470   Ostracism of Themistokles.

469   Victory of League fleet under Kimon over Persians at Eurymedon. End of effective Persian threat to Aegean.

466–5   Condemnation of Themistokles and flight to Persia.

465–463   Revolt of Thasos from League crushed.

462 Athenian expedition under Kimon to help Sparta against Messenian revolt (465–460).

?463 Aeschylos' *Supplices* – hints of democratic propaganda.

462 Ephialtes and Perikles curtail powers of Areopagos.

461 Ostracism of Kimon.

460–445 War between Athens and Sparta (first Peloponnesian War).

457 Aeschylos' *Oresteia* – a justification of Ephialtes and Perikles.

449 Formal peace signed with Persia (peace of Kallias).

443 Beginning of supremacy of Perikles.

432 Athenian defensive alliance with Korinth's colony Kerkyra.

431 Invasion of Attika by Peloponnesian army. Beginning of second Peloponnesian War.

429 Death of Perikles.

?428 Publication of Herodotos' *Histories* (largely written earlier).

425 Kleon acquires near-Periklean prominence.

424 Aristophanes' *Knights* (attack on Kleon) and (?) 'Old Oligarch' (philosophical analysis of Athenian democracy).

422 Death of Kleon.

421 Peace of Nikias between Athens and Sparta.

420 Intrigues of Alkibiades in Peloponnese leading to Athens/Argos alliance.

418 Battle of Mantinea between Argos with her allies (including Athens) and Sparta – peace of Nikias not officially broken.

416 Athenian sack of Melos.

415 Euripides' *Troades* – a condemnation of war.
Athenian expedition to Sicily.

414 Sparta resumes hostilities against Athens.

413 Athenian disaster in Sicily.

412 Euripides' *Helena* – post-disaster escapism.

411 Oligarchic revolution at Athens (The Four Hundred).
Expulsion of the Four Hundred and institution of moderate
oligarchy (The Five Thousand).

410 Restoration of full democracy.

405 Final defeat of Athens at Aigospotamoi.

404 Surrender of Athens and installation of Spartan-backed
oligarchy (The Thirty).

403 Restoration of democracy and general amnesty.

Bibliography

If a book has been published both in Britain and in the United States both publishers are listed, the British one being named first. Dates are of first publication.

General

The best short history of Greece is still that of J. B. Bury, *History of Greece*, revised by R. Meiggs, Macmillan/St Martin's Press, 1951; more up-to-date but less satisfying as an introduction to the subject is N. G. L. Hammond's *History of Greece*, Oxford University Press, 1959. A. R. Burn offers a good general account of the period 700–500 BC in his *Lyric Age of Greece*, Arnold/St Martin's Press, 1960. Volumes III–V of the *Cambridge Ancient History* (12 vols.), Cambridge University Press/Macmillan, 1923–39, cover our period more fully with chapters by various hands of very unequal merit.

On the arts see R. M. Cook, *Greek Painted Pottery*, Methuen/Quadrangle Books, 1960; A. W. Lawrence, *Greek Architecture*, Penguin, London, 1957; G. M. A. Richter, *Archaic Greek Art*, O.U.P., 1949, and *Sculpture and Sculptors of the Greeks*, O.U.P., 1950; M. Robertson, *Greek Painting*, Zwemmer/Skira, 1959; C. T. Seltman, *Greek Coins*, 2nd edn, Methuen/Humanities Press, 1955; J. Boardman, *Greek Art*, Thames and Hudson/Praeger, 1964.

1 Failure and achievement

For the details of the Athenian constitution see C. Hignett, *A History of the Athenian Constitution*, O.U.P., 1952. For an appreciation of its working, A. H. M. Jones, *Athenian Democracy*, Blackwell/Praeger, 1957, chs. 3 and 5; A. W. Gomme, *More Essays in Greek History*, Blackwell, Oxford, 1962, pp. 177ff; M. I. Finley, 'The Athenian Demagogues', *Past and Present*, Vol. 21, 1962, pp. 3ff. My view of the Athenian Empire is basically that of G. E. M. de Ste Croix, *Historia*, Vol. 3, 1954, 1ff.

All the Athenian writers mentioned have been well translated in readily available editions: Aeschylos, some Sophokles and Euripides, Thucydides and some Plato in the Penguin Classics series; all of these completely, with Euripides and Aristophanes, in the Loeb Classical Library and the Everyman Library; a modern version of Aristophanes by various hands, *The Complete Greek Comedy*, edited by W. Arrowsmith, Univ. of Michigan, 1961–, is now appearing (*Acharnians*, *Birds*, *Frogs*, *Clouds*, *Wasps* already published); excellent too are Dudley Fitts' *Lysistrata*, *Frogs*, *Birds*, *Thesmophoriazusae*, Faber, London, 1955–60. The tragedians have been well served by D. Grene and R. Lattimore in *The Complete Greek Tragedies*, C.U.P./Chicago, 1959.

2 Aristocratic society

In *The World of Odysseus*, Chatto & Windus/Viking, 1954, M.I.Finley gives an excellent account of Greek society in the tenth and ninth centuries BC. Some details are filled in by A.Andrewes in *Hermes*, Vol. 89, 1961, pp. 129ff; *JHS*, Vol. 81, 1961, pp. 1ff; and his inaugural lecture *Probouleusis*, O.U.P., 1954. L.Gernet's article, 'Droit et prédoit', *L'Année Soc.*, 1948–9, pp. 21ff gives an illuminating account of one vital aspect of this primitive world. The *Iliad* and *Odyssey* of Homer are translated by E.V.Rieu in the Penguin Classics (passages quoted in the text are in his translation); Hesiod by Evelyn White in the Loeb Classical Library. For a short appreciation of Hesiod see H.T.Wade-Gery, *Essays in Greek History*, Blackwell, Oxford, 1958, pp. 1ff.

3 Economic expansion

T.J.Dunbabin, 'The Greeks and their Eastern Neighbours', *Hellenic Soc.*, *Supp. Papers*, 1957, and J.Boardman, *The Greeks Overseas*, Penguin, London, 1964, give brilliant accounts of eighth-century expansion. See also J.M.Cook, *The Greeks in Ionia and the East*, Thames and Hudson/Praeger, 1962, chs. 4–5.

Archilochos and other early elegiac poets (Tytraios, Solon, etc.) are translated by J.M.Edmonds in *Greek Elegy and Iambus*, Loeb Classical Library, 1931, to whose edition references are given in the text; lyric poets in his *Lyra Graeca*, Loeb, 1922–7. For a more reliable presentation of the Greek see *Anthologia Lyria Graeca*, 3rd edn, Teubner, 1951–; cf. C.M.Bowra, *Early Greek Elegists*, O.U.P./Harvard, 1938, and *Greek Lyric Poetry*, 2nd edn, O.U.P., 1961.

For the account of the word 'tyrant' which I modify (p. 79–84) see A. Andrewes, *The Greek Tyrants*, Hutchinson/Harper, 1956, ch. 2. For the date of hoplites, Andrewes, *op. cit.*, pp. 31ff. The evidence, old and new, is re-examined by A.Snodgrass in *Early Greek Armour and Weapons*, Edinburgh U.P., 1964.

4 Revolution in Korinth

For tyranny in general see A.Andrewes, *The Greek Tyrants*; for Kypselos see ch. 4. Older views in P.N.Ure, *The Origin of Tyranny*, C.U.P./Macmillan, 1922; H.T.Wade-Gery in *Cambridge Ancient History*, Vol. III, C.U.P./Macmillan, 1925, ch. 22. For the growth of Greek science and philosophy, etc., see J. Burnet, *Early Greek Philosophy*, 4th edn, Black/Macmillan, 1930; L. Pearson, *Early Ionian Historians*, O.U.P., 1939; T. A. Sinclair, *A History of Greek Political Thought*, Routledge, London, 1952.

5 Revolution in Sparta

Professor Andrewes discusses Sparta in ch. 6 of *The Greek Tyrants*, implying a late date; cf. H. T. Wade-Gery, *Essays in Greek History*, pp. 37ff. For an early date see N. G. L. Hammond, *JHS*, Vol. 70, 1950, pp. 42ff; W. den Boer, *Laconian Studies*, Amsterdam, 1954, Part I. For the compromise, G. L. Huxley, *Early Sparta*, Faber/Harvard, 1962, ch. 3; W. G. Forrest, *The Phoenix*, Vol. 17, 1963, pp. 157–79. P. Roussel, *Sparte*, 2nd edn, Paris, 1960, and H. Michell, *Sparta*, C.U.P., 1952, give more general accounts of this strange state and its institutions. The sad effects on the tradition of the later worship by Greek conservatives of the Spartan constitution have been excellently described by F. Ollier in *Le Mirage Spartiate*, (2 vols.), Paris, 1933 and 1943.

6 Revolution in Athens – Solon

Again see Andrewes, *op. cit.*, ch. 7. Also W. J. Woodhouse, *Solon the Liberator*, O.U.P., 1938; K. Freeman, *Work and Life of Solon*, Milford, New York, 1926. Andrewes' revised view of the origin of hektemorage which I have largely adopted here will be set out in a book to be published shortly. He has with great generosity allowed me to present a very brief and somewhat modified account of it here.

The fragments of Solon's poems are translated by Edmonds, *Greek Elegy and Iambus*, in the Loeb Classical Library; for an appreciation see C. M. Bowra, *Early Greek Elegists*, O.U.P./Harvard, 1938, ch. 3. The two chief sources for his work, Aristotle's *Constitution of Athens* (the authorship is sometimes disputed but without any good reason) and Plutarch's *Life of Solon* are translated, Aristotle by K. von Fritz and E. Kapp, Hafner, New York, 1957, and by H. Rackham in the Loeb Classical Library; Plutarch by B. Perrin, also in Loeb.

For further detail of constitutional matters see C. Hignett, *History of the Athenian Constitution*, O.U.P., 1952, ch. 4 (with whom I disagree on many fundamental points); H. T. Wade-Gery, *Essays in Greek History*, Blackwell, Oxford, 1958, pp. 86–115; G. E. M. de Ste Croix, *Essays* (to be published shortly).

7 Tyranny in Athens

Again see Andrewes, *op. cit.*, ch. 9. Hignett, *op. cit.*, ch. 5.

8 The reforms of Kleisthenes

On Kleisthenes see Hignett, *op. cit.*, ch. 6 and Wade-Gery, *op. cit.*, pp. 135–54. For details of his *trittys* system, D. M. Lewis, *Historia*, 1963, pp. 22ff; C. W. J. Eliot, *Coastal Demes of Attika*, University of Toronto Press, 1962. For the view that Kleisthenes was a disinterested reformer and for an important study of ostracism, G. E. M. de Ste Croix, *op. cit.*

9 From Kleisthenes to Ephialtes, 508–462 BC

For the years between 508 and 462 see Forrest, *Classical Quarterly*, 1960, pp. 221ff, where I try to justify the very brief and dogmatic account of Themistokles and his opponents given in the text; for constitutional details, Hignett, *op. cit.*, chs. 7 and 8; Wade-Gery, *op. cit.*, pp. 170–200; on Aeschylus, K. J. Dover, *JHS*, Vol. 77, 1957, pp. 230ff; E. R. Dodds, *Proceedings of the Cambridge Philological Society*, 1961.

On the expansion of Persia see A. T. Olmstead, *History of the Persian Empire*, C.U.P./Chicago, 1948; on the Persian Wars, A. R. Burn, *Persia and the Greeks*, Arnold/St Martin's, 1962.

10 The great debate

Some useful light is thrown on the political debate in the late fifth century by A. Fuks, *The Ancestral Constitution*, Routledge, London, 1953; more by the 'Old Oligarch' Xenophon, *Scripta Minora*, tr. E. C. Marchant, Loeb Classical Library; and by Aristophanes' *Knights* and *Wasps*.

Acknowledgments

Some few of my debts to other historians are acknowledged in the bibliography; many more are not. Here again I can name only one or two, Sir Maurice Bowra, Professors H.T.Wade-Gery and A.Andrewes, Messrs G.E.M.de Ste Croix and T.C.W.Stinton. To them and many other colleagues, in Oxford and elsewhere, of whose ideas, wittingly or unwittingly, with or without permission, I have 'taken toll without restraint', I am deeply grateful.

My thanks are also due to Mr T.Stalker-Miller who drew the maps and to Mrs Catherine Porteous who collected the photographs. For special help in providing photographs I am also indebted to Doctor L.H.Jeffery, Mrs Jane Rabnett, Professor P.Amandry, Mr A.Snodgrass and Mr B.B.Shefton.

Acknowledgment is due to the following for the illustrations (the number refers to the page on which the illustration appears). Frontispiece, 8, 19, 151, 152–3, 205 David Beal; 10, 71, 87, 95, 120 The Louvre, photos Josse Lalance & Cie; 16, 17, 20, 88–9, 200, 201, 222 Agora Excavations, American School of Classical Studies, Athens; 23, 29, 211 Ashmolean Museum; 24–5, 28, 40–1, 47, 56, 57, 59, 65, 69, 70, 80–1, 82, 83, 84, 85, 96, 99, 107, 117, 118, 136, 140 photo John R. Freeman, 141, 157, 162, 184, 185, 187, 188 photo John R.Freeman, 223, 225, 233, 234 British Museum; 27, 32 Staatliche Museen zu Berlin; 35 Aufnahme des Kunsthistorischen Museum; 37 J.Allan Cash; 61, 179, 206 National Museum, Athens; 68 Deutsches Archäologisches Institut, Athens: 74 Akropolis Museum; 76 British School of Archaeology, Athens, drawing by R. V. Nicholls; 91 French School of Archaeology, Athens; 92 A.Snodgrass; 106 National Tourist Organisation of Greece, photo V. and N.Tombazi; 126 P.Amandry; 139 Giraudon; 165 Archaeological Museum, Istanbul, photo L.H.Jeffery; 190 B.B.Shefton; 230 Alison Frantz.

W.G.F.

Index

World University Library

Some books published or in preparation

Economics and Social Studies

The World Cities
Peter Hall, *London*

The Economics of Underdeveloped Countries
Jagdish Bhagwati, *Delhi*

Development Planning
Jan Tinbergen, *Rotterdam*

Leadership in New Nations
T. B. Bottomore, *Vancouver*

Key Issues in Criminology
Roger Hood, *Durham*

The Sociology of Communication
J. L. Aranguren, *Madrid*

Education in the Modern World
John Vaizey, *Oxford*

History

Ancient Egypt
Werner Kaiser, *Berlin*

The Emergence of Greek Democracy
W. G. Forrest, *Oxford*

Mahomet and the Great Arabian Conquests
Francesco Gabrieli, *Rome*

The Crusades
G. Widengren, *Uppsala*

The Medieval Economy
Georges Duby, *Aix-en-Provence*

The Ottoman Empire
Halil Inalcik, *Ankara*

The Rise of Toleration
Henry Kamen, *Edinburgh*

The Left in Europe
David Caute, *Oxford*

Chinese Communism
Robert C. North, *Stanford*

History and Sociology of Religion

History of the Christian Church
W. O. Chadwick, *Cambridge*

Monasticism
Dom David Knowles, *London*

Judaism
Rabbi J. Soetendorp, *Amsterdam*

The Modern Papacy
K. O. von Aretin, *Göttingen*

Sects
Bryan Wilson, *Oxford*

Language and Literature

A Model of Language
E. M. Uhlenbeck, *Leyden*

French Literature
Raymond Picard, *Sorbonne*

Russian Literature
Ronald Hingley, *Oxford*

Satire
Matthew Hodgart, *Sussex*

The Arts

Primitive Art
Eike Haberland, *Mainz*

The Language of Modern Art
Ulf Linde, *Stockholm*

Aesthetic Theories since 1850
J. F. Revel, *Paris*

Art Nouveau
S. T. Madsen, *Oslo*

Academic Painting
Gerald Ackerman, *Stanford*

Palaeolithic Art
P. J. Ucko and A. Rosenfeld, *London*

Modern Drama
Peter Szondi, *Göttingen*

253

254

Psychology and Human Biology

Eye and Brain
R. L. Gregory, *Cambridge*

The Ear and the Brain
Edward Carterette, *U.C.L.A.*

The Variety of Man
J. P. Garlick, *London*

The Biology of Work
O. G. Edholm, *London*

Bioengineering
H. S. Wolff, *London*

Psychoses
H. J. Bochnik, *Hamburg*

Child Development
Philippe Muller, *Neuchâtel*

Man and Disease
Gernot Rath, *Göttingen*

Zoology and Botany

Animal Communication
N. Tinbergen and J. M. Cullen, *Oxford*

Mimicry
Wolfgang Wickler, *Starnberg*

Migration
Gustaf Rudebeck, *Stockholm*

The World of an Insect
Remy Chauvin, *Sorbonne*

Biological Rhythms
Janet Harker, *Cambridge*

Lower Animals
Martin Wells, *Cambridge*

Physical Science and Mathematics

Mathematics in Science and Daily Life
H. Freudenthal, *Utrecht*

The Physics of Low Temperatures
K. A. G. Mendelssohn, *Oxford*

Particles and Accelerators
Robert Gouiran, *C.E.R.N., Geneva*

Optics
A. C. S. van Heel, *Delft*

Waves and Corpuscles
J. A. E. Silva and G. Lochak, *Paris*
Introduction by Louis de Broglie

Earth Sciences and Astronomy

Anatomy of the Earth
André de Cayeux, *Sorbonne*

The Electrical Earth
J. Sayers, *Birmingham*

Climate and Weather
H. Flohn, *Bonn*

The Structure of the Universe
E. L. Schatzman, *Sorbonne*

Applied Science

Words and Waves
A. H. Beck, *Cambridge*

Operational Research
A. Kaufmann, *Sorbonne*

DATE DUE

NY 12 '93			